Guide to the wines of
Bordeaux

PAMELA VANDYKE PRICE

PITMAN

PITMAN PUBLISHING LIMITED
39 Parker Street, London WC2B 5PB

Associated Companies
Copp Clarke Ltd, Toronto
Fearon-Pitman Publishers Inc, Belmont, California
Pitman Publishing Co. SA (Pty) Ltd, Johannesburg
Pitman Publishing New Zealand Ltd, Wellington
Pitman Publishing Pty Ltd, Melbourne

© Pamela Vandyke Price, 1977

First published in Great Britain 1977

Text set in 10/11 pt Photon Baskerville, printed by Photolithography and bound in Great Britain at The Pitman Press, Bath

ISBN 0 273 00936 2 (paperback edition)

For
Helen
who loves claret as I do
and who has been of so much help to me
with this, and many other books

Acknowledgements

So many friends and firms have helped me during the years I have been studying the region of Bordeaux and its wines that it is not possible to thank all of them by name. The French Government Tourist Office and S.O.P.E.X.A. in London have provided constant assistance, including introductions to many authorities in Bordeaux, notably M. Louis Desgraves of the Municipal Library, whose own books are outstanding and who gave me the privilege of seeing the first edition of the *Essais* corrected in Montaigne's own hand. Among those who have been unsparingly generous with their time and hospitality are: Ronald Barton of Château Langoa; Martin Bamford, M.W. of Château Loudenne and all his colleagues there; John Davies, M.W. of Château Lascombes; M. Alain Querre and his family; Edouard Cruse; Bruno Prats; Raymond Dupin; Henri Mähler-Besse; and Guy Schÿler. To Baron Elie de Rothschild of Château Lafite-Rothschild I owe particular thanks, also to Baron Philippe de Rothschild of Château Mouton-Rothschild. The establishments of Cruse, Cordier, Eschenauer have been most helpful and, in Great Britain, I am extremely grateful to the firms of H. Sichel & Sons, Hedges & Butler, O. W. Loeb, Laytons and to the late Ronald Avery of Averys of Bristol, with whom I was several times fortunate enough to go tasting in Bordeaux. David Peppercorn, M.W., has been kind enough to help me on many occasions with the wines we both love so much, and William Bolter in Bordeaux, who read this book in manuscript, made a number of valuable suggestions from his great knowledge of the place and its wines. Most of all I must admit my indebtedness to Maison Sichel, Bordeaux, who, more than any others, were responsible for introducing me to claret and who have helped me in many ways throughout the years; members of the firm, past and present, have unstintingly given their encouragement and assistance, and especially to John Salvi, M.W., I owe my thanks for an outstanding exposition as to how claret is made. To all these and many others who have contributed to enabling me to write this book my gratitude and affection can only be briefly expressed, but they will, I trust, know that this is as much their book as it is mine.

Pamela Vandyke Price *1976*

Contents

Cover photograph by courtesy of the French Tourist Office

1

The Bordeaux Region

Bordeaux is the fourth greatest city in France and that country's third most important port. The city and the region around it are variously known, either as 'the Bordelais' or the Gironde, from the mighty river that within its estuary, splits into the rivers Garonne and Dordogne, and gives its name to the *département* or province today. The Roman name for the Gironde was Aquitania, or 'land of waters', because of these great rivers and this became Aquitaine in medieval times, when it was one of the most important duchies in France. The name is still used today, rather picturesquely, just as the inhabitants are often referred to as Girondins, a word that became prominent in history when the leaders of the French Revolution gave their collective name of Girondins, referring to the origin of most of them, to their party.

The countryside is pleasant, often charming, but not spectacular, and it is often by-passed or rushed through by tourists in search of the more obviously beautiful neighbouring regions of the Charente and Deux Sèvres to the north, the valleys of the Dordogne and Lot to the east, and the Pays Basque and Pyrenees to the south. There are some beautiful churches and impressive castles, though such works of art usually need seeking out, for the region seldom publicises them more than discreetly. The resorts, whether on the sea coast, the river banks or the large inland lakes, are simple and quiet, where families go for rest and relaxation rather than tourists for amusement.

Bordeaux itself is a conglomeration as assorted as its inhabitants: there are gigantic docks and harbour buildings, modern industrial zones and nineteenth-century factories; huge, stark blocks of offices, flats and public buildings, plus a vast exhibition park and hall that looks like something from a lunar landscape, with an expanse of man-made lake surrounded by hotels of international appearance and resources. There are miles of plain grey suburban streets, as shabby, shuttered and closed to the outsider as in any French provincial town, a chunk of a Roman amphitheatre, mighty remnants of medieval palaces and churches once famous throughout Christendom, alleys that are still virtually fifteenth-century slums, within a stone's throw of quays, squares and avenues of delectable eighteenth-century elegance. It is an odd city set in an odd landscape. There are numerous books on Bordeaux, Aquitaine and various aspects of art, architecture and history in the region written in French, and of course it is included in all the standard guide books dealing with this part of France, and receives fair mention in some English books too. But, as far as I know, none of the more general guide books display any particular interest in the subject that has made Bordeaux famous in a particular way—its wine—and those who have written specialised books on this particular subject have only intermittently considered the needs of the traveller. So, after some experience of advising prospective visitors where to go and what to see and of taking round tourists who share this specialist interest, I am compiling this portable publication that may be of service.

For one thing that brings thousands of business visitors to Bordeaux, without their knowing much if anything of its history, the commodity that conjures up images of glamour, wonder and delight in the minds of those who will never even get to Aquitaine at all, is wine.

Even the total abstainer could not avoid noticing, during the most rapid visit, that this is not only a town in a wine region, but also a true wine city. Anyone arriving by air will, from the time that the southbound plane is announced as being over the Cognac region, see the candlewick-like regular tufting of the vineyards and, as the plane turns over the Gironde and is above the Médoc, the geometric precision of the rows of vines is interspersed by a variety of buildings, turreted, battlemented,

Local colour

with towers like witches' hats, or sloping roofs and ivy-covered walls like English country houses—the *châteaux* of some of the great estates. No longer does the visitor see millions of casks, the *barriques de Bordeaux*, lying on the quaysides, waiting to be swung into the holds of the freighters; today, ships are packed with more accommodating and tougher containers, which often look rather like vast petrol cans. No longer is there the club-like atmosphere at the two big hotels in the centre of the city, where the wine trade and their guests would forgather, where the telephonists knew the telephone number of anyone who demanded *"Donnez-moi la maison"* ("Get me the office") and where thousands of pounds worth of business might be done while heads of firms were having coffee or sharing a restorative bottle of Vichy water. Today, although some hotels still have their regular wine trade visitors, it is the luxurious establishments outside Bordeaux, with pools and gardens and tourists from all over the world that accommodate visiting businessmen—unless, of course, you are fortunate enough to be lodged in one of the châteaux arranged for the reception of guests. But Bordeaux is still predominantly wine orientated, however much her fortunes may be augmented by the establishment of other businesses.

The taxi driver will still discuss vintage prospects with the passenger, the woman in the *tabac* kiosk will comment on the weather in relation to the condition of the vines, the hairdressers and boutiques will be immediately aware of the needs of clients who have arrived for some specific wine dinner or reception, and ask for a report on it; the *garagiste* will be interested in a proposed route among vineyards and probably advise as to some "little place where one doesn't eat too badly", while the staff at the finer restaurants may well be acquainted with who visited which property when—and what they said about the particular wines. Indeed, I have spent a Saturday up in the Médoc visiting and tasting at several estates, lunching at another one, and then had some of my comments repeated to me at a restaurant where I was dining in Bordeaux in the evening; I have taken the Sunday evening plane back to London, walked in to a restaurant for lunch on the Monday and had a member of the wine trade from the north of England quote back my Sunday morning remarks to me! The associated meanings of the word 'grape-vine' are all relevant when wine is the subject, especially the wine of Bordeaux.

Climate and Landscape

The vine, a curious plant, gives of its very best where it has to fight for existence. It can yield well in places where soil and climate favour vegetation and pleasant, even very good wine can result. But great wine comes only from the outer limits of regions within which the vine can grow—and the vine is the type of plant that can grow in places where no other vegetation useful to man except the olive can exist. It is when the vine has to struggle to yield at all and when it needs all the assistance that man can give it, both in its cultivation and the use of its fruit, that great wine results. The situation of Bordeaux is such that the grapes that make the finest red wines can have—if the weather is right—enough sun to ripen them but not too much so that they are coarsened by having to adapt to the great heat; and where there is sufficient coolness for the white wines not to lose their freshness and lack the acidity that, even when they are slightly or very sweet, must be present if they are to avoid being flabby. The climate of the region is in general temperate, with a tendency to warm, even hot summers, with quite a lot of moisture and mists in the autumn and winter, possibly some frost in the winter and early spring, and some gentle rain even during the summer. In many ways, it is not unlike a slightly exaggerated version of the climate of southern England, with more heat in summer and slightly softer winter rains and fewer winds.

Except for the St. Émilion vineyard, the landscape is only slightly undulating and indeed many people might say that the Médoc was virtually flat; but the slopes are there, even if barely noticeable to the eye. This is important, not merely for the drainage of the vineyard, which should enjoy a certain amount of both aeration within and protection from the surrounding landscape, but also because the subsoil, from which the deeply plunging tap roots of the vines draw their nourishment, is also varied. A vineyard that is completely flat, on a plain, may give good wine but I have never known a great wine come from such a vineyard. At the other extreme, a vineyard that is on the crest of a steep hill will usually make wine that is less high in quality than one that is halfway down or two-thirds up.

Farmers will probably endorse this in relation to other crops (for example, the new potato crop is always better from halfway up the slope in the south of England). So the climate of Bordeaux, temperate, with quite a lot of moisture and usually a certain amount of heat in the summer, is good for certain of the grape varieties that make fine wines. It should be stated, however, that it is precisely their ability to produce grapes that make fine wines that can result in these particular grape varieties being rather vulnerable to certain forms of disease as well as natural hazards, such as frost and hail, so that they need extra care, like any thoroughbred variety of anything that lives.

Although the Gironde is quite an agreeably green countryside, the soil is not rich, except for some patches on the right bank of the river; you will see few market gardens and no meadows of waving corn, no lush pastures nourishing dairy cattle, and gardens, although they will be carefully tended to provide a variety of vegetables and are brilliant with roses in the summer, are seldom as variegated with flowers and shrubs as the British visitor might expect. This is poor land, with small forests and scrubby heaths in many regions and, to the south, the vast pine forests of the Landes; this was virtually a desert until, towards the end of the eighteenth century, the engineer Nicholas established plantations of pines to arrest the invasion of drifting sand. These pine forests have not only held the earth in place but they are a valuable source of revenue for their owners, not just for timber, but because of the resin they yield, and the odd pots to catch the drippings of this resin, affixed to the sides of the trees, may be seen in all regions. The workers, who used to go on stilts, in order to reach the resin deposits placed high up on a tree trunk and to navigate the marshy ground in the Landes, are now more inclined to use Land Rovers and may only be picture postcard figures to the casual traveller. Some do, however, still work with the aid of these curious stilts.

So it is poor country, with sand, gravel, and some reddish limestone in certain areas. But this is precisely the type of terrain that makes for the production of fine wine. This is what the vine likes. Visitors to a vineyard will note the orderly rows, free from weeds, but with stones thick on the ground—and kicked back on the vineyard from the paths by anyone showing them round. These stones make for good drainage, they hold the heat, which they will reflect upward on to the bunches of ripening grapes. The grapes themselves will be protected by the pruning of the shoots of the vine so that the leaves shelter the fruit from the most direct rays of the sun at its fiercest; the sand or the curious sandy clay which the traveller should handle and feel, gives lightness and elegance to the wines.

Every wine region is different and the great classic wine grapes now are grown in many parts of the world. But, however good the wine they make, it is, in my opinion, only in the Bordelais that certain of them give of their very finest. But then, the maturation of a vineyard is as important as the maturation of a vine stock, and the greater Bordeaux vineyards have been making fine wines for nearly two hundred years, or sometimes more.

Bordeaux—an Important Junction

The geographic situation of Bordeaux and its vineyards is another reason why it is of such importance. Bordeaux itself has been settled by human beings since before records existed. The reason for this is that it is the lowest place on the Garonne river at which a crossing can be made. The availability of a ford was obviously of the greatest importance before the building of bridges. It is not always realised today how much people depended on rivers and, later, canals, for conveying goods and people, and a place where both could be ferried across the water from one main region to another was certain to be the site of a town. Indeed, although the river is still very wide, it is astonishing to relate that the first bridge was only built across the Garonne in the early nineteenth century (1816–21), and until very recently in the postwar period there was only this one bridge for pedestrians and traffic, plus a railway bridge!

A river with an estuary such as that of the Gironde provides the advantages of a navigable stream and the extent of a small sea; the Gironde is salt for quite an extent of its estuary, and therefore the facilities for fishing were considerable. In some ways it was one long natural harbour, providing a place of refuge for sea-going craft and affording those who lived along the banks valuable access to trading routes. The boats that came down the Dordogne and Garonne could put up in the Gironde, even though the pirates, who at times inhabited the islands and the mouth of the estuary, were hazards almost as great as those of the Atlantic ocean outside. But as soon as roads began to be built, Bordeaux stood at an important junction: look at a map and you will see that the route down from Germany through northern France and eventually to Spain lies naturally through the heart of the Gironde, and the roads from the mountains of the interior of France and the south, including the waterways, converge on this point at which traders could set forth by sea for northern countries. "There had to be a city there" said Camille Jullien, one of the great historians of Bordeaux.

But the situation of the place meant that, as well as trade passing through the region, trading stations themselves would eventually be established there and, as well as people being able to leave from Bordeaux to go to other countries, so they could come to Bordeaux from places where their own trading prospects might not be so bright and, increasingly, where political or religious pressures might make it difficult for them to live. The traders and merchants may have pioneered the establishment of the prosperity of Bordeaux, but the scholars, the religious refugees and teachers, some soldiers of fortune, aristocrats out of favour in their particular milieu, all found possibilities for the future and an agreeable way of life in the Gironde. During the Middle Ages, it was possibly the main stopping point on the great pilgrim route to Santiago de Compostella, which was rated second only to that to Jerusalem in medieval Christendom, when the Pope declared that Santiago pilgrims achieved remission of all their sins. Pilgrims might come to Bordeaux overland from north or east, or disembark there having made the sea voyage, to proceed through the remaining dreary landscape to the Spanish frontier.

In more recent times, nineteenth-century political, economic and religious oppression have resulted in many illustrious names of foreign extraction establishing great houses in the world of Bordeaux wine; the city has been a refuge for politicians, and even for the entire French Government. Small wonder, then, that these influences from every side should have contributed to an area where the attitudes of mind of many nations are still quite evident, even when the families or firms concerned have been established for a century or more, and where the technical as well as the philosophic and economic contributions made by the arrivals have resulted in wines of such variety.

Red and White

At least 500 square miles of the Bordeaux region are under vines. This is approximately divided between red and white, something that will probably suprise those who think of Bordeaux as predominantly a red wine region. But the significant thing is that at least two thirds of all these wines are *Appellation Contrôlée* (see page 113) and of a category that may be described as good to very good, with a substantial proportion being great. There are more great wines produced in the area than in any other region of France as regards quality and, for those who love them, they are the supreme wines of quality.

How is it possible, then, to guide a visitor with perhaps only a short time to spend—or, in these days when the love of wine has resulted in the establishment of study groups of students of wine being established outside France, give an introduction to those who may have little hope of ever visiting the great vineyards—in the space of a short book? What I am trying to do here is to indicate the important characteristics of the region, the interesting historical events that link the world of wine with many episodes in English history, and to give a commentary for the visitor who is looking at vineyards and wines, wishing to know a little more about both. The last word on Bordeaux can never be said, and the list of books at the end of this one will indicate how much more has already been written, but I hope that this may be an introduction.

Don't try to read this book straight through: consult the section with which you are immediately concerned, whether this is tasting, concerns the wines of a specific region, the history, the particular vine variety or something to do with the legislation that controls labelling. Use what people have written in the past as interesting and possibly helpful guidelines, remembering that, like medical or legal textbooks, every book written on wine is out of date within a year or even months of its appearance, so do not make up your mind once and for all that a particular statement is right, any more than you should make up your mind once and for all as to your reactions towards a particular type of wine. This is a book to be used, the way one uses a friend whose advice one asks before going somewhere and whose companionship may be helpful on the way.

It is an old saying that "everyone has two countries, his own and France". As far as lovers of fine wines are concerned, everyone must have one other particular homeland; my own has always been Bordeaux. There can be no greater delight for the lover of wine than to introduce and increase knowledge of his or her particularly preferred wine—and I hope that this may be the justification for my writing this book.

2

Bordeaux
and its Wines in History

The Gironde is rich in prehistoric as well as historic remains and treasures, but although Burdigala, as it then was, exported quantities of wheat, for which Gaul was an important source of supply at the time of the Roman Empire, Julius Caesar does not mention vine cultivation in his 'Gallic War' and historians assume that the only wine the inhabitants of Aquitania would have drunk was that brought from the Mediterranean. There is nevertheless a theory that the Phoeniceans, in their trading voyages to Cornwall and the south of England, made use of the port of Bordeaux and therefore it is just possible that wine, even, maybe, a little of it made in Aquitania, came to Britain even before Roman times.

Bordeaux in Roman Times

By 100 B.C., however, there were a number of vineyards established in France (Gaul as it was then), of which the most important seems to have been that around Narbonne. The Roman Senate tried to protect their national crops of olives and vines by excluding all the other producers from certain benefits to which the Italians of the period were entitled for cultivating these crops. Tolosa (Toulouse) became an important centre for the expeditions of the wines of the Narbonne vineyard and, along the route that these cargoes of wine would have proceeded, mostly by river, there have been found remnants of amphorae, some of them going as far as Burdigala in one direction and down to Pompeii in the other.

The Bordelais were drinking wine, even though this might have been made in or round Pompeii, at the time of Cicero (106–43 B.C.) and, gradually, an increasing number of growers in the province of Gaul began to plant vines and make their own wines. Saintes, which had formerly been the capital of Aquitania, had to yield in importance to Burdigala, which became the centre of government towards the end of the second century A.D., although its position was disputed by Poitiers in subsequent years. Increasingly, the governors of Burdigala

wielded enormous power, as may be seen by the career of
Agricola, who, thanks to the Roman historian Tacitus, has a
well documented biography, and who became Governor of
Aquitaine in A.D. 74 under the Emperor Vespasian.

The city became large, prosperous, with an aristocratic élite
and there were many public buildings, of which only fragments
remain today; the gigantic Palais Gallien, capable of seating
15,000 people, built in the third century A.D., indicates
something of the quality of urban life at this time. The poet
Martial (*circa* A.D. 40–104), a shrewd and worldly Spaniard,
noted the bustling character of the city. It became the junction
of some of the most important routes of Gaul. There was a
Greek colony, which established a tradition for instruction in
grammar; other settlers of which records remain from the
second century include Spaniards, Bretons, Celts, Belgians and
Germans, as well as the Roman-born citizens. Interestingly,
there was a considerable amount of trade between Burdigala
and Treviris (Trier), and it seems to have been about this time
that Bordeaux wine began to be exported in significant quantities, the Germans bringing cloth down the rivers Mosel and
Rhine and selling it in London, loading up there with cargoes
of chalk which they brought down to Burdigala. There they
reloaded their vessels with wine, to sell in Belgium. The city was
truly cosmopolitan and one of the historians calls it "a little
Rome". The Bordelais even had a mother goddess, particularly
protective towards them—Tutela, usually represented by a
plump lady holding a cornucopia, often decorated with vine
leaves. There is an altar dedicated to her in A.D. 224 by a
merchant of York and Lincoln, who thanks her for his fortunate voyage. The Piliers de Tutelle, the first Roman monument recorded as existing in Bordeaux, stood at what is now
the north-west corner of the theatre; this impressive colonnade,
of which only drawings remain, was unfortunately pulled down
in 1677, when the great fort of the Château Trompette was
being enlarged.

The richness of the city and the increasing threat of bar-
barian invasions caused the erection of substantial walls around
the central part, a large rectangle, running approximately from
the Quai de la Bourse up to the Rue de Ramparts, and from the
Place Rohan down the Cour d'Alsace et Lorraine and thence
virtually along what was then the river bank to the Place de la
Bourse. This concentration of the city was necessary, because
the northern barbarians had begun to be a serious menace,
sacking the city in A.D. 276.

In the fourth century Bordeaux wine inspired one of the
greatest poets of the time. Ausonius, a Bordelais by birth, a
scholar famous throughout the Empire and later Prefect of
Gaul and a Consul, was tutor of the young man who was to
become the Emperor Gratian. He also taught the equally

famous and distinguished Girondin, Paulinus of Nola (353–431), who was also born at Bordeaux. Ausonius' correspondence with Paulinus, and his verses on Paulinus' absence in Spain and subsequent adoption of a type of monastic Christianity, are some of the most touching documents that survive from this period. The story of Ausonius and Paulinus appears in Helen Waddell's *The Wandering Scholars* and their verses, together with her exquisite translations, in *Medieval Latin Lyrics* (both books originally published by Constable; subsequently in paperback by Penguin).

Ausonius loved the good things of life and praised the wines of his homeland, considering that their quality was the reason for the very long lives of both his grandfather and father. He refers to the local oysters, and his fondness for fishing, revealed in his poem about the Moselle, show his love of the sport in the waters of his homeland, also his fondness for hunting and entertaining his friends. He took great delight in sending the local specialities to friends who lived far away, and appreciated receiving presents from them, including olive oil from Spain. He possessed at least more than one villa outside Bordeaux itself and, as he remarks on the noise in the city, it was natural that he should seek the tranquillity of country life: unfortunately there is a great deal of disagreement as to exactly where these villas were, although some probable sites have been found. Possibly the best memorial to Ausonius, however, is the great vineyard that bears his name in St. Emilion (see page 51).

The University of Bordeaux, with its origins dating from a tradition of scholarship and lively minds as early as the third century, is seen, therefore, to derive from a mixture of cultures and to have drawn freely on the resources of the later period of the Roman Empire. The region was receptive to Christianity, and by the end of the fourth century Christians were numerous there; records that survive state that pilgrimages were made from Bordeaux to Jerusalem in 333. Bordeaux became the seat of the bishopric, and the influence of Paulinus of Nola and Ambrose of Milan was considerable in the region. The region is rich not only in the prehistoric and Roman remains that are still being discovered, but in the burial places of Christians of the fourth century. By then, Bordeaux was gaining in importance due to its position on the pilgrim route to the shrine of Santiago (St. James) de Compostella and the church of St. Seurin (Seurin or Séverin was one of the early bishops of Bordeaux) is particularly rich in such remains.

The Dark Ages

After the sack of Rome in 410, the city seems to have maintained both its independence of spirit and its commercial importance. It became the Gothic capital of King Euric in 476, when the Empire was centred on Byzantium and prior to the

Merovingian epoch, but the region still retained its Roman traditions, because, when anyone crossed the river Garonne, they were said to be 'going to the Romans'. The northern barbarians, both by land and in their pirate ships, became an increasing menace. However, under Charlemagne, King Clovis managed to defeat Alaric, King of the Goths, in 507, and Bordeaux became the official capital of Aquitania. This was an evil time, and although many of the great religious houses were established then, acting as hospitals, schools, hostels for travellers and places of research for scholars, life in general became more difficult and communications perilous.

In 580 there was a bad earthquake, which destroyed many of the houses in the city and the weather seems to have been very bad: wolf tracks were observed in the vineyards, and during the winter the wolves even came into the city itself and devoured the domestic dogs. When King Clovis died, his heirs quarrelled and fought with the Dukes of Aquitaine, as the province had now become, and at the same time there were serious menaces from the south. The Saracens invaded France from Spain in 731 and over-ran the country as far north as the Loire. Eudes of Aquitaine and Charles Martel defeated them decisively near Tours, but the threats of piracy by odd bands of Saracens remained for a long while. Writers on Bordelais gastronomy accredit the survival of dishes such as couscous and kebabs to this distant period, but seems more probable that their existence in the Gironde dates from the arrival of the '*pieds noirs*' (French from Algeria) in the past twenty years. The Emperor Charlemagne, however, brought peace to the region around 778, though there is a tradition that the sword and the olifant or horn of his nephew, Roland, and the bodies of Roland and the Peers of France (who fought the disastrous rearguard action at the pass of Roncesvalles, in the Pyrenees) are deposited at St. Seurin. This is a stirring story, although as historically improbable as the Song of Roland* itself. What is certain is that Charlemagne took a considerable interest in the Bordeaux wine trade; his interest in vine growing is perhaps better known in relation to the Rhine and Burgundy, but in fact he had influence on the Bordeaux trade as well, prohibiting the transport of wine in leather bottles, and stipulating that only ironbound casks might be used. He also suggested that wine of especially good vintages could be stored in amphorae. The advantage of the amphora, often kept in the earth for coolness, is obvious when you remember that, by this time, the use of cork, known to the Romans, had been forgotten: new wine was therefore obviously superior to old, while it kept its freshness. Exposure to air and especially to warmth would either turn the

---

* The song that was sung by William of Normandy's minstrel Taillefer as he rode against the Saxons at Hastings in 1066.

wine or make it taste as unpleasant as wine subjected to similar ordeals will today.

Times were still troubled for Bordeaux, which was captured by Scandinavian pirates and fiercely attacked by the adventuring Normans in 844. They had to be paid off by Charles the Bald of France, and when his son, Louis, became King of France in 866, Aquitaine became a simple duchy, united to Gascony in 1039.

The Dukes of Aquitaine reigned, like kings, over a vast countryside, extending from the valley of the Indre, just south of the Loire, down to the Pyrenees, and, eastwards, almost to the edge of Burgundy. It was not a particularly civilised time and Bordeaux had scarcely recovered from the ravages of the pagan invaders. But the culture of the vine survived, and, at the turn of the tenth and eleventh centuries, a commentator describes "Opulent Aquitaine . . . as pleasant as nectar thanks to its vines". The Blaye vineyards certainly date from at least this period if not earlier, as do Entre Deux Mers, Vayres, possibly the Graves and Sauternais, as well as the Premières Côtes, also around Bordeaux itself, including vineyards belonging to certain parishes actually in the city. Even up in the Bas-Médoc, where wine was being made at Soulac at least as early as the twelfth century. If you walk about in Bordeaux today, in the central part around the Cathedral, between the space around it and the Cours de l'Intendance, remember that all the churches in this part of Bordeaux had their own vines, and in fact one street in the parish of St. Christoly was called the Rue des Treilles (*treille* means vine arbour or simply vine—hence the English word trellis) which existed until the fourteenth century and ran along what is now part of the Rue de Grassi. Vines were grown literally under the columns of the Piliers de Tutelle and on the city walls; and the Church of St. Seurin owned a number of vineyards, and was particularly important. The fact that a tax was levied on the sale of wine in the urban borough of St. Seurin indicates that there was a considerable amount of business going on in the wine trade and in fact this caused much quarrelling between various ecclesiastics, each anxious for his own products to make the most profit.

Eleanor of Aquitaine

In 1137 there was a wedding at the Cathedral of St. André between the heir to the King of France and one of the most remarkable women of the middle ages—Aliénor (Eleanor), daughter and heiress of Duke William X of Aquitaine, who had recently died in somewhat mysterious circumstances while on a pilgrimage to Santiago de Compostella. Eleanor is one of the most fascinating personalities of the Middle Ages, but, in English history, she has perhaps been unfairly eclipsed by Queen Elizabeth I; she is certainly as important and influential.

Some of her adventures included escaping out of a castle window into a snowbound countryside when she was well into what we should nowadays describe as middle age, creating a deliciously enigmatic scandal by her conduct on a pilgrimage to the Holy Land, presiding over the Courts of Love instituted by one of her daughters at Poitiers* and, when she was a really old woman, escorting her future daughter-in-law, Berengaria of Navarre, across Europe to Cyprus for her wedding to Richard Coeur de Lion. It is a pity there are only two adequate biographies of her, by Amy Kelly and Régine Pernoud; she was certainly the most glamorous woman of her time, a worthy granddaughter of Duke William IX of Aquitaine, who was the first of the troubadours and wrote delicious love songs. The poets of her own day wrote about her when she might fairly have been considered as getting on in years:

> Were the whole world mine,
> From the sea to the Rhine
> I'd give it all if the Queen of England
> Lay in my arms.

If you want to see one of the few representations of Eleanor's face that survive, go to the Cathedral of St. André in Bordeaux and look up at the columns on the north wall, west of the pulpit: there is the head of someone supposed to be a bishop, although it might well have been Eleanor's first husband of whom she said "I thought to have married a man, not a monk", and then there is her face, beautiful and assured. Eleanor and Louis were crowned as Duke and Duchess of Aquitaine at Poitiers, on their way back to Paris, but before they reached it Louis' father died, and they were King and Queen of France.

Unfortunately, although Eleanor gave Louis two daughters, she had no sons, and the marriage was in many ways unsatisfactory. St. Bernard of Clairvaux, who, as those who remember his denunciation of Peter Abelard will understand, was hardly a tactful adviser to the King, was no help to her either. There is no reason why he should have been—he had excommunicated her father in somewhat dramatic circumstances. At this time, too, he was having trouble with an unruly family from Anjou, of whom, referring to their supposed descent from the marriage of Count Fulk the Black with the Fairy Melusine, he

---

* The Courts of Love were rather like aristocratic discussion groups at which men and women debated matters affecting the conduct of both sexes in relation to each other in love and/or friendship. Their influence on the literature of the time was considerable; pragmatically they provided a special civilising influence on the young nobility, who were sent to attend the Courts as a means of acquiring good manners, courtly behaviour and a knowledge of music, poetry, and other arts. The room in which they were held is now the waiting room of the Law Courts—a place of such light and beauty that it seems as if the original courtiers had only just gone out of the door.

said "From the devil they came—to the devil they will go". This was the family of Count Geoffrey, who, because of his habit of wearing a sprig of broom (*planta genista*) in his bonnet, were known as 'Plantagenets'. Eleanor and Louis were divorced in 1152 and she retired to her own Duchy, marrying the young Henry Plantagenet, considerably her junior, in 1152 in Poitiers. Two years later he was King of England.

The English had, hitherto, only bought moderate amounts of Bordeaux wine, but now they began to drink it in vast quantities, in spite of the competition from the King's native Anjou. When it is remembered that the English crown at this time included Normandy, Brittany, Maine, Anjou, Guyenne and Gascony, in addition to Aquitaine itself, the prosperity of Bordeaux, centre of the English Government in France, will be realised being as of enormous importance. The Palais de l'Ombrière, of which now only the great gate (Porte de Cailhau) remains, looks out on the quayside and is still referred to as "The palace of the Kings of England". For several centuries it is said that the arm of the archer who killed Richard Coeur de Lion (favourite son of Eleanor, to whom she gave the Duchy during one of the many quarrels of the young princes and their father) was suspended from one of the walls opposite. Richard II, called "of Bordeaux" may have been born here, or in the castle at Lormont, across the river.

Shipping the Wine

In order to get the wine to the English ports, particularly to London, while it was still in good condition, an enormous fleet of two hundred or more ships would arrive in the Garonne just after Christmas each year. They would then race back, even though they had to pay various taxes at the points passed along the French coast. Because of the pirates who lurked at the top of the Garonne estuary and round the Brittany coast, some of the ships began to carry arms. The huge casks used were tonnes or tuns, each holding 252 gallons; they occupied 62 cubic feet of space in the hold of the ship—in this sense, 'tonnage' became the standard measurement for the capacity of a sea-going vessel.

Regulations about making the wine were becoming stricter, notably the *Ban des Vendanges*, or proclamation of the vintage, the announcement made when people were allowed to start picking, so that no unscrupulous grower could steal a march on his competitors and risk selling a wine made from unripe grapes. Wines from other parts of France, coming up by road and river, were also exported through Bordeaux, the city exacting a tax on these and prohibiting their despatch before the local wines; the Jurade of Bordeaux, the governing body, insisted that wines coming from outside the specific Bordeaux vineyard could not be kept within the city, but had to be stored outside the city walls. Because the merchants wanted these

stocks of wine to be as near to the river as possible and even as
far up the river as possible so as to save time when they could
eventually be loaded, the stocks began to be congregated in the
region of an ancient charterhouse, a little north of Bordeaux
along the river; as the area became more built-up, this Pavé des
Chartrons became the Quai des Chartrons—which is the centre
of the Bordeaux wine trade today. Many Englishmen owned
both property in Bordeaux and vineyards too, but the Jurade
passed legislation to the effect that anyone who was actually
selling wine had to be a resident of the city; they also defined
the limits of the vineyard.

English Influence

The importance of Bordeaux increased, and the citizens
enjoyed many special privileges: they were even permitted to
travel and trade freely in France, although they were of course
inhabitants of what was often an enemy country. Much business
was done with the English court (the French court drank
Burgundy, both because the wine was nearer to Paris and
because the great Dukes of Burgundy were valuable allies
against the English) and contemporary accounts are full of
arguments about prices, requests for payment and, occasional-
ly, settlements: King John owed Bordeaux 1,080 marks for wine
and Henry III paid off only 600 marks of this debt. The English
were frequently defaulting customers of the Bordelais. But
English influence remained very strong in the region, and (as
Philip Oyler has shown in his wonderful book *The Generous
Earth*) there are still many traces of the English occupation in
words, manners and such everyday terms as pet names for
domestic animals.*

English power in Aquitaine began to wane by the fifteenth
century. It will be appreciated that people who had been ac-
customed for over 200 years to look on a slice of France as their
own, and whose rulers spoke French at court, would certainly
find objections to relinquishing what they had come to look on
as 'their' kingdom. The Bordelais, shrewd merchants and
negotiators that they have always been, were particularly adroit
in playing off the French against the English at the time when
theirs was somewhat debatable land in between the two powers:
in 1406 the French were besieging Blaye and the Bordelais had
to appeal for help to Henry IV of England. However, before he
could send help, the Bordelais Jurade commandeered the wine
fleet, at that time in the river, and even shot one of the English
captains who was obstinate about relinquishing his ship. Acting
on their own initiative, they then sent fire ships among the
French fleet stationed off St. Julien and utterly defeated them.

---

* Geoffrey Chaucer (1343?–1400) may have visited Bordeaux, for he was the
son of a vintner. He certainly travelled in France, and refers to "Bordeaux
town" and "La Rochelle" in *The Pardoner's Tale*.

In the Agincourt war, 1415, Henry V sent down to Bordeaux for both guns and wine when he was besieging Harfleur.

Bordeaux was besieged by three French armies in 1443 and spies were constantly infiltrating the city to try and persuade the Bordelais to surrender. War, for the nobility, was still rather a courtly game, and the Bordelais seem to have been particularly hospitable to anyone taken prisoner; for example, after the battle of Poitiers, the French King who had been captured was most lavishly entertained by them. But it was becoming increasingly difficult for the Bordelais to hold out against the French. Although the Archbishop of Bordeaux, Pey Berland, who had grown up in the vineyards, actually went to England to try and get help from Henry VI, by 1451, Dunois, the companion in arms of Joan of Arc, captured Blaye and advanced on Bordeaux, so that the Jurade were compelled to negotiate. They did pretty well for themselves out of the subsequent agreement, maintaining all their civil liberties and most of the '*privilèges*' (remission of taxes) they had previously enjoyed. The war finished, on this occasion, in a pageant-like way: heralds went to the tops of the towers of the city walls and ceremonially cried for help from England. Then the Bordelais and the French processed outside the city and staged a mock battle, after which the French were admitted and everyone celebrated peace.

As so often happens, however, the Bordelais had not been quite as clever as they had expected, and they were left with enormous stocks of wine on their hands, because King Charles VII of France was traditionally a Burgundy drinker. Nor could they sort out the ownership of many estates in the Gironde. So, when the French king didn't keep his promise to remit the taxes on Bordeaux, the city opened its gates to the Duke of Bedford, sent out to be mayor by Henry VI of England. This followed the custom of the time when the mayors of Bordeaux were appointed from London (French historians have it that the actual appointment continued to be made for several centuries, although I can find no trace of this in London records),

The end of English rule in Aquitaine came in 1453, 299 years after the accession of Henry II to the English throne. Sir John Talbot, Earl of Shrewsbury, was defeated at the Battle of Castillon, the memorial to which may still be seen on the roadside. The French besieged Bordeaux and might have sacked it, but an epidemic in their camp forced them to disperse. The French King would in fact have paid the remaining English to leave, but they had scuttled their ships, so had no option but to stay where they were. The English wine trade had perforce to transfer its business to the port of Rouen—which could also handle Burgundy—but, with peace, English wine buyers were allowed to come back to the Gironde, although they had to leave their arms at Blaye and could only go into the vineyards when accompanied by an authorised guide. The Scots, however, were granted some additional privileges "because he (the Scot) hath always been an useful confedearte to France against England" and had "right of pre-emption or first choice of wines in Bordeaux; he is also permitted to carry his ornance to the very walls of the town". The English had looked on Aquitaine as their own for a long time; indeed, the British royal standard bore the fleur-de-lys of France until 1803.

The Sixteenth and Seventeenth Centuries

During the religious wars and social upheavals of the sixteenth century many foreigners arrived to settle in Bordeaux, enriching the city's life. A great deal of building and expansion went on, the marshes outside were drained, and the Fort du Hà, the remains of which are now a prison, and the gigantic Château Trompette, on what is now the vast space of the Quinconces, were erected as fortifications. In the same century, the great essayist Michel de Montaigne was mayor of Bordeaux; his town house was in the Rue de la Rouselle, in the Salinières, the region devoted to those who were trading in salt fish. Montaigne's house, a rather modest building, was where he lived until he resigned all his civic appointments in 1570 and retired to live at the Château de Montaigne, away from the town, which was often plague-ridden at the time. The Château itself was burned down in the nineteenth century, but Montaigne's study and library were left intact. The dumpy little tower with his bedroom and workroom, the mottoes that he inscribed on the beams of the ceiling and the little window through which he could see into the chapel so as to be present at the services are all still there, and if you apply to the present owners, M. and Mme. Mähler-Besse, you may be able to fix an appointment to see them. What Montaigne says about tolerance, moderation, and the pleasures of talking with friends and enjoying a quiet life in the country may still be taken as representative of the attitude of a civilised Bordelais today.

Meanwhile the wine trade was increasing and approximately 5,400 tons of Bordeaux wine were sent to London each year during the reign of Queen Elizabeth I. The wines were quite heavily taxed, and encountered considerable competition from those exported from La Rochelle (a virtually vanished vineyard, now) and the Loire, but their popularity never waned. In 1556, a licence had been given to import as much as 10,000 tons, an enormous amount in relation to the population of the time. In 1597, it is recorded that, in the Port of London, there were 26 ships from Bordeaux, one from Rouen, and 34 from the Low Countries, all engaged in bringing in the new vintage.

In 1615, King Louis XIII was married in the Cathedral of St. André to the Infanta of Spain, the beautiful Anne of Austria. The independent Bordelais, as might have been expected, were not particularly royalist; they were loyal to neither Louis XIII nor his more authoritarian son, Louis XIV. The citizens not only took sides with those who revolted against the *Gabelle* or salt tax, and with the anti-monarchists of the Fronde (they even appealed for help to Cromwell in 1649), but also gave shelter to a number of religious and political refugees, especially those Protestants who were suffering as a result of the fall of La Rochelle and the revocation of the Edict of Nantes.

Although Louis XIV was a gigantic eater, he seems to have been a moderate drinker and, although the satyr-like Duc de Richelieu, Governor of Bordeaux, attempted to popularise Bordeaux wines at the Court, he appears to have had only moderate success. The Duc de Richelieu's house was in the Cours de L'Intendance, on the site of the nineteenth-century building that now is the shop of the Belle Jardinière; this was formerly the town house of the Pichon family, where Louis XIV was received when he passed through Bordeaux on his way to his marriage with another Infanta of Spain at St. Jean de Luz.

Bordeaux might have had a champion in another unusual woman, Madame de Maintenon. She was probably born in Bordeaux, in the Château Trompette itself, where her father had been imprisoned for joining one of the conspiracies of the King's uncle, Gaston d'Orléans (he had previously killed his wife having found her with a lover) and where he courted and married the daughter of the prison governor.

The wine trade prospered and expanded in export markets, and references to specific estates began to appear: Samuel Pepys mentions the wines of "Ho Bryen" (Haut Brion), a property which the English philosopher John Locke visited in 1679. Pontac's was established in London in an attempt to popularise the white wines of Blanquefort, and in John Evelyn's Diary there is an account of Evelyn meeting M. de Pontac, the son of the Mayor of Bordeaux. Brandy began to be distilled in the area, though, like the former merchants of high country wines, the distillers were compelled by decree to keep their stills outside the walls of the city. Rather oddly, Bordeaux did not possess more than a few ships, the Dutch and English being the most prominent in the port. At about this time it received its name of *Port de la Lune*, due to the new-moon-like curve of the river.

An Era of Prosperity

In the first fifty years of the eighteenth century the population of Bordeaux doubled in size and the wine trade continued to flourish, although the Methuen Treaty of 1703 gave the advantage to the wines of Portugal on the British market.* By this

* Wine in bottle could develop without deteriorating, and, English glassware being superior at this time, English bottles much sought after. In 1723 Peter Mitchell of Dublin set up the first bottle factory in Bordeaux and by 1790 there were five factories in the city, producing 400,000 bottles a year.

time the old city walls had virtually disappeared, the quaysides were extended, the Quai du Bacalan being begun in 1690, and at last the city began to develop its own wine fleet, sending 75 ships to England in 1729. This was in many ways the great century for Bordeaux: the outstanding man of letters is Montesquieu, Baron de la Brède (1689–1755), a great thinker and philosopher from a family of the region, whose study may still be seen in the beautiful Château de la Brède, which seems to float on the moat that surrounds it.

Château de la Brède

In spite of many difficulties because of wars between nations, Bordeaux wines continued to be in demand and the city's prosperity is reflected in the glorious squares, avenues and many public buildings that were erected under the famous Intendant, Tourny. The Place de la Bourse, the Grand Théâtre, the Place Jean Jaurès, the building that is now the Hôtel de Bordeaux, and the Allées de Tourny are just a few. Combes, a pupil of the Parisian architect of the Duc de Richelieu (Victor Louis, designer of the Paris Opera), designed many fine buildings, including Château Margaux and its *chais* (wine stores). You have only to walk along the Allées de Tourny, turn down to the river and make for the Quai des Chartrons or, in the other direction, along the quayside to the Place de la Bourse, to see what an elegant city eighteenth-century Bordeaux must have been; note, too, the un-French names on many of the streets (such as Place Finwick), and the variegated nationalities implied by the names of the firms with their premises along the riverside.

Perhaps the houses in the Cours Xavier Arnozan are the most beautiful of all, but those on the quaysides are especially interesting, because they were at once the business premises and homes of the old wine trade families. The cellars are just below ground, so that the wines in cask could be rolled up a ramp, across the quay and loaded directly on to the waiting vessel; the offices were on the ground floor, sometimes extending to higher floors, and the living quarters of the family would originally have been on the top storeys. The beautiful doors, wrought iron balconies and plaster mouldings may be shabby today, but they indicate a past of fantastic prosperity and a gracious way of life.

The outbreak of the French Revolution put a stop to the expansion of this beautiful city. The Quinconces—second in size only to Moscow's Red Square— is where the old Château Trompette used to stand. It was stormed and demolished at the outbreak of the Revolution, as was the Bastille in Paris. The monument to the liberty-loving Girondins is now in the centre of the square. Under the Terror, the guillotine was set up in what is now the Place Gambetta and 300 citizens of Bordeaux were executed. The unfortunate Girondins who hid in one of the caves at St. Émilion were discovered and later guillotined in Paris.

The English wine merchants and their families who remained were interned, but none of them was executed. Indeed, trade seems not merely to have been maintained but developed, especially with the Indies and Macao, particularly under the supervision of Balguerie Stuttenberg, a powerful merchant prince whose name is commemorated by the long Cours de Balguerie Stuttenberg where so much business is done in Bordeaux today. Not for nothing had the the the Bordelais Montesquieu said: "Let nothing stop the march of commerce!" But Napoleon's attempted blockade of the British Isles resulted in the accumulation of vast stocks of wine at the port.[*]

In Search of Claret

The British went on drinking claret however. The 'Auld Alliance' had created a particular market for the wine of Bordeaux in Scotland, and throughout Great Britain it was a mark of loyalty to the Stuart cause to drink claret, which had been popular at the court of King James II. There are accounts of people sending wines from various parts of Europe to Great Britain as substitutes for claret, especially when the court of Charles II and fashionable London discovered the delights of Champagne. In 1691, a ballad *In Search of Claret* by Richard Ames described how he went from tavern to tavern in London trying to get a drink of claret, but everywhere was offered port, or, even in those establishments that had long wine lists—wines from Spain, Italy, and Portugal, but no Bordeaux.

[*] At this time nearly all wine was handled in bulk, and such bottles as were used were irregular, easily broken in transit, and nothing could be done to put right a wine that had deteriorated because of lying about in the heat on a quayside or in the hold of a ship.

In 1721 the export of Bordeaux totalled 34,138 tuns, more wine than had ever been despatched from the port since the early fifteenth century. The Low Countries, Germany and the Baltic were taking substantial quantities, as well as Great Britain. But the high excise duty on French wines in the late eighteenth century was prejudicial to them: for example, in 1789, customs records of the port of Bristol show that the French wines coming in paid £25.4s.0d. a tun, but Portuguese only £16.16s.0d. Whereas in 1723 Bordeaux wine exports had represented 69 per cent of the total production, by the end of the eighteenth century exports accounted for only 14 per cent: the aristocrats and wealthy bourgeoisie in France, like their British equivalents, continued to drink claret and other Bordeaux wines, but many of the middle and certainly the lower classes were unable to afford them. The wealthy and discriminating drinkers in Great Britain were buying estate wines but, even between 1787 and 1789, the English trade dropped from 26 per cent of the Bordeaux wine exports to 4·7 per cent.

By then, other wines and even brandy were being blended with those of Bordeaux to give them a higher alcoholic strength, dark colour and general gutsiness. A great deal of the Bordeaux wine trade went through Guernsey, and there was a tremendous amount of business done with Irish drinkers, as witness the exports to Ireland of 1,285 tuns in 1786, when the exports of Bordeaux to England were only 225 tuns.

Napoleonic Times

Smuggling had been carried on during all the wars of the eighteenth century, but during the Napoleonic blockade it became large-scale. Wine taken from ships captured at sea was added to the amount smuggled, which enabled some British drinkers to continue drinking Bordeaux. Napoleon I, accompanied by Josephine, went to Bordeaux in 1808, when he was obliged to make the city a loan in order to stabilise the situation caused by the loss of trade to the port because of the war. It is supposed to have been his idea to build a boulevard around the city, and he was the first to begin to make plans for building a bridge across the Garonne, because a considerable township had grown up on the other side of the river. Napoleon proposed to build a wooden bridge, but nothing immediate was done about this. Eventually, between 1816 and 1821, the bridge was built, but of stone—hence its name, the Pont de Pierre. It was the only bridge for pedestrians and ordinary traffic until the 1960s.

Bordeaux does not seem to have been very pro-Napoleon. The wealthy bourgeoisie were doubtless right to be hesitant about welcoming him, in spite of the revolutionary example of the early Girondins. In March 1814 Marshal Beresford appeared at the gates of the city (which the exiled King Louis XVIII had proclaimed as "the faithful") and the city yielded. The then Governor, the Duke of Angoulême, had married the only surviving child of the wretched Louis XVI, who, it is perhaps interesting to know, was defended at his trial by a citizen of Bordeaux, Romain de Sèze. He must have been a brave man to undertake the task, especially as he had an aristocratic name.

The Princess, Madame Royale, was a courageous and vigorous woman. She inherited the title after the death of both her parents and an aunt and the strange disappearance of the little boy who had become Louis XVII on the execution of his father. When Napoleon escaped from Elba, she attempted to rally the region to the cause of the Royalists. The British ship *The Wanderer* came to take her off from Pauillac to safety when the citadel of Blaye hoisted the tricolour, and it looked as if the area would go over to the Napoleonic force. But after Waterloo the Duke and Duchess of Angoulême returned to Bordeaux.

It was also after the battle of Waterloo that Sir Charles Palmer, who had served in the Peninsula Campaign and had come to know the region during his subsequent leave, bought the Château de Gasq, a vineyard in the Médoc to which he devoted his fortunes, and to which he gave his name of Palmer. Unfortunately, he was not a good businessman and although the vineyard produced wines of increasingly fine quality, it virtually ruined him. The 'P' on the medallions above the doorways today does not refer to Palmer but to the Pereire family, who bought the estate and erected the building in the middle of the nineteenth century.

The past 150 Years

During the last hundred and fifty years Bordeaux has continued its tradition of being a place of refuge for exiles. The painter Goya, in exile from Spain, died at 57 Cours de l'Intendance in 1828. A native of Bordeaux was another painter, Rosa Bonheur (1822–99). In 1871 the novelist and playwright Victor Hugo brought his family to the city to attend the National Assembly of which he was a member, and lodged at 13 Rue St. Maur. Here, after he had resigned from the Assembly and was given a farewell dinner to his son and daughter-in-law in a restaurant, news was brought in that the son for whom they had been waiting had died of an apoplectic fit in a cab outside the Café de Bordeaux. Hugo admired Bordeaux very much: "take Versailles, add Antwerp, and you have Bordeaux".

Other visitors include Florence Nightingale, who as a young woman made a visit to Blaye, and Thomas Adolphus Trollope, brother of the novelist Anthony Trollope, who, in the 1840s, travelled round the south-west of France. In a coach ride from Bordeaux to the Dordogne ferry he had the company of a wine

merchant who was going up to the depot at Paris-Bercy; having
got this man off what was evidently a boring conversation
about the slave trade, Thomas Adolphus says "He told me
several anecdotes of prices almost incredible given for choice
wines; but mentioned none so high as that which another
merchant told me of, upon another occasion. He had recently
sold, he said, a thousand bottles of Château Margaux to the
Emperor of Russia at 36 francs a bottle. It was 34 years old, and
had a bouquet, which its owner assured me scented strongly the
whole of a large room as ever it was opened; nor had its age
destroyed a particle of its colour, flavour or even strength."

Another visitor in 1838 was the French novelist Stendhal,
who said that Bordeaux was divided into five different towns,
including "English merchants who keep to themselves
exclusively". There were also Protestant merchants, merchants
from Mexico, Cuba and Peru, merchants from Mauritius and
India, young men who came from the south of France, Per-
pignan, Cognac and Limoges, and, of course, the descendants
of the early merchants of Bordeaux. Stendhal found the people
attractive, musical and great gamblers, and he describes them
as being an "obvious mixture of the Iberian, the Cimbrian, and
the Gallic races. Beautiful eyebrows." As for a typical Bordeaux
day, he says "A Bordeaux businessman sees his wife only at
meals. On rising, he goes to his office; at 5 o'clock he goes to
the Exchange which he leaves at 6 and goes home for dinner. At
half-past seven, he is at his club where he spends his time
reading newspapers, talking with his friends and gambling. Not
until midnight does he go home and often not till two o'clock
in the morning. The women spend their evenings completely
alone. . . . Many married men keep a mistress whose house
they visit from 7 to 9 in the evening. . . . Those young women
are much happier than the married women, for every day they
spend at least two hours with the man who prefers them."

In the Franco-Prussian war of 1870–71 the French Government was transferred to Bordeaux, a circumstance which was
repeated from September to November 1914 at the beginning
of World War I, and again in June 1940, after the fall of France
in World War II. In June 1917 the first American troops to
enter the First World War were landed at the Pointe de Grave,
exactly where Lafayette is said to have embarked in 1777 to go
to the assistance of the American colonists in the War of
American Independence.*

Bordeaux is still a place of enormous intellectual importance: writers, thinkers, scientists and technicians all benefit
from the excellent resources of the University. The dramatist
Jean Anouilh was born in Bordeaux, although it is a pity that,
in view of the fascinating true history of Aquitaine, his play

---

* This event is also claimed to have taken place at Pauillac.

about Becket and Henry II should be totally inaccurate.

Another world-famous literary figure of the Gironde was François Mauriac, whose novels and plays give some idea of the tightly closed society of the bourgeoisie of Bordeaux and the Landes at the beginning of this century and before 1939; one of his early novels, *Preséances*, descibes the curiously parochial society of the nevertheless multi-racial *noblesse de bouchon,** the members of the many great wine trade families, which are virtual dynasties, often complicatedly intermarried. But Mauriac saw much of the society he knew so well with rather too clear a vision for comfort: to this day, if you want to throw a verbal squib into the highly civilised conversation around a Bordeaux lunch table, ask the host if he does not agree that *Preséances* is still a pretty accurate picture of life in the wine trade!

But perhaps Mauriac should have the last word on Bordeaux, which has been called "the kitchen and the chamber-pot of France". He admits "I cannot take a long view of Bordeaux, I am too involved in it. I associate myself with its very stones. 'The countryside of the heart', to use the phrase of Amiel, is, as far as Bordeaux is concerned something even more—the countryside has become one's very being and it is impossible to be impersonal about it." He was talking about Bordeaux in general. I think that what he said applies to the wines as well as to the countryside.

---

* Literally, 'the bottle cork nobility'.

3

What the Wines Are

The Bordeaux region makes still table wines: red, dry white, a little rosé or pink wine; also sweet white wines, and some sparkling white wines. The most important of these, in relation to the wines of the world, are the red wines and the sweet whites, and many people would assert that the greatest of the reds are the greatest red wines in the world, also that the finest of the sweet whites are unique and outstanding.

Perhaps the most important thing to remember about the red wines, however, is that, although a huge range is produced, from cheap to costly, a higher proportion of really fine wines are made in the Gironde than in any other single vineyard region of France. About two-thirds of all Bordeaux wines are A.O.C. (see Appendix 4).

It is important to know in general terms how the wines are made, so that your enjoyment of them can be increased by understanding how and why they are as they are. Also, anyone visiting a wine estate will want to get some idea of what is going on, what is meant by several of the processes referred to, and what the various pieces of equipment in the *chai* (store) or *cuvier* (vathouse) are for. Wine making is a scientific as well as a picturesque process; certainly even in the most modest establishment in the Gironde you will look in vain for a musical comedy chorus of merry peasants singing and dancing while treading in a vat! But the reality can be just as fascinating.

The Sparkling Wines

These play a comparatively small part in the Bordeaux wine scene. They are white, fairly dry and slightly full, and can be pleasant celebration drinks. The significant thing about them is that it was in Bordeaux that they began to be produced in a particular way for a large-scale market. Early this century, a Monsieur Charmat perfected a method for making sparkling wines without subjecting them to the costly and lengthy Champagne process. He made them in a sealed vat (*cuve close*), instead of letting them complete their fermentation in bottle, like

Champagne; this procedure was found well suited to wines that do not require long-term maturation. Monsieur Charmat's firm originally used white Bordeaux wines, but nowadays their scale of production is vast, and they have moved out of the region and make up their blends from wines from many areas. But it was the Charmat method and the Charmat firm that were responsible, at the beginning of the twentieth century, for producing the best-selling Veuve du Vernay in Bordeaux.

The Pink Wines

These are made either by allowing the skins of red or black grapes to remain in contact with the fermenting must (grape juice before it becomes wine) for just long enough to impart some of the colour, or else by blending red and white wines. As most grape juice and certainly all the juice of Bordeaux black grapes is pale at the outset, rather like grapefruit juice, it will be appreciated that the very deep-toned skins of the various black grapes (always referred to as black rather than red) only need to remain in contact with the must for a short time.

CLAIRET

Clairet is a term that is also used to signify a pink wine in this region—but it will be a rather deeper pink than the ordinary rosé. Bordeaux rosé and Bordeaux clairet are not, in fact, exactly the same, although they may appear so to the drinker. But clairet is an interesting name, for it was the origin of the word 'claret' by which the red wines of Bordeaux are known throughout the English-speaking world, although in the U.S.A. the wines are possibly more often referred to as 'Red Bordeaux'.

Clairet, in fact, means a light coloured wine—*clair* is French for lightness or paleness when referring to colour. In former times, before the skill of the wine maker enabled at least drinkable wine to be made in most years, the pale, possibly wishy-washy wines of an indifferent year in Bordeaux could be given a more definite and attractive colour and possibly a more robust flavour by the addition of some of the much darker-toned wines from the hinterland, which were known generally as 'high country' wines. Among these was the famous 'black wine' of Cahors. The Bordeaux vineyard area was once much less extensive, and consisted mostly of the *palus* or river banks in the Médoc, and the difficult-to-cultivate Graves and St. Émilion vineyards. Up to well into the nineteenth century customers would specify how they wanted their Bordeaux wines 'Improved'. This meant the addition of various dark, full wines from other regions, including Spain; 'Hermitaged' Bordeaux was Bordeaux with an admixture of the Hermitage of the Rhône—considered a superior blend to those made with cheaper additives. But today 'clairet' may be thought of as a pink wine, rather deeper-toned than usual. Claret, the unadulterated wine of Bordeaux, is red—though, as any comparison will show, it is usually a lighter, more tawny-tending red than the purplish, deep crimson of many other southern red wines.

Red Wines

THE VINTAGE, AND MAKING THE WINE

It has sometimes been said that these are the most natural wines of all the classics. Even today, when they are tended with all the skills available to the contemporary maker of wine, there are still some mysteries, happenings that may make nonsense of preconceived calculations, sudden changes of character that not even the laboratory can explain, certain failures when all seemed set for success—and, fortunately, many more pleasures and triumphs than might ever have been expected.

First, the bunches of ripe grapes are picked by hand, then transferred from the baskets carried by the vintagers to big ones, which are loaded on to a lorry. Until fairly recently, this would have been a horse-drawn cart, or even one pulled by oxen, for the animal manure was useful to the vineyard and the animals could pass easily through the vineyard tracks. The beasts would be well-groomed and often adorned with elaborately-decorated harnesses, but this kind of vintage scene is rare today.

Each grape variety is picked separately, because some varieties ripen early, others late, and it is the responsibility of the man in charge to deploy the bands of vintagers to the appropriate sections of the vineyard, which may itself be parcelled out in small portions and not all in one place, each section ripening at a slightly different time because of location. Then the loaded lorries take the grapes to the *cuvier* (the building that houses the vats, or vathouse), where they are tipped out into a reception area, which usually looks rather like a shallow tank. (Grapes coming in for processing at a co-operative will first be weighed, so that the growers supplying them can be paid according to how much they produce.)

Grapes must be handled as soon as possible after picking, otherwise they may begin to rot. Within half an hour they should be stripped off their stalks. Nowadays, this stripping is usually done by a mechanical destalker, called a *égrappoir fouloir*: the grapes are tipped or shovelled onto what usually looks like a revolving drum, that whirls the bunches around, so that the grapes come off and are soon pulped. This, it must be emphasised, is the only 'pressing' that the grapes receive. They are taken off their stalks (which are collected to serve as a form of manure) and, while passing over the *égrappoir*, are broken up and, eventually, crushed into a mass of pulp. There is no point in subjecting them to actual pressure by a weight; this would release too much colour from the skins and, by breaking the pips, would make the wine bitter and harsh. Anyone who wants to see huge beam presses or giant screw presses that once required the strength of several men to turn will have to look for them in museums and old prints.

However, in some *cuviers* there is the tradition of the *égrappage à main*, or hand destalking, which is carried out by shovelling the grapes onto a large wooden table with holes in it, which looks rather like a piece of slatted garden furniture. A skilled team of three or four men rub the grapes across these slats, so that the pulp is broken, the juice runs through and the men end up holding wiry-looking bunches of stalks. This is very hard work and difficult to justify in purely economic terms. But the method means that at no time do the grapes come into contact with anything metal (even the spades with which they are shovelled are wood) and, if the workers can keep pace with the arriving loads, it is still thought, even by many of those who have had to abandon *égrappage à main*, that the resulting wine may be somehow finer, and more traditional in style. One of the estates where the process can still be seen is Château Palmer.

FERMENTATION

The grape juice and pulp is pumped into the fermentation vat, the mass of skins forming what is called a *chapeau* or 'hat' on the top of what is not yet wine, but *mout* ('must'). In former times all vats were huge wooden vessels, but nowadays you may see tank-like vats, lined with various substances including glass, vitreous enamel or stainless steel, or a vat may be wholly stainless steel. Because of the geographical situation of Bordeaux it is not necessary to enclose or in any way restrict the process of fermentation, whereby the must is acted upon by the yeasts, which convert the sugar in the grape juice into alcohol and transform the must into wine: the fermentation proceeds without the help of any added chemicals or extra yeasts.

This is not the place to describe the process of fermentation in detail, but essentially the juice of the crushed grapes is converted into wine by the action of wine yeasts, which are in the atmosphere of any vineyard, and work upon the 'bloom' of the grapes, seen on the skins, and feed on the sugar in the juice. If the temperature rises to a certain height, then the yeasts cannot work—they are killed by the heat, and serious problems assail the wine maker. If the temperature remains low, then the yeasts never start to work, or, if it drops, then they also stop working—just as happens when the domestic kitchen uses yeast to make bread or cakes and pastry. A great deal of damp, similarly, will inhibit the working of the yeasts, and rain will wash off the bloom from the grapes on which they feed.

So it is important to appreciate that the comparatively

temperate climate of Bordeaux is not only conducive to
favourable conditions for the wine, but, at vintage time, to
good wine making: the atmosphere then is usually dry and
warm, without being dangerously hot in most years or suddenly treacherously cold, or disastrously wet and damp. Though
the uncertainty of the Bordeaux climate can still ruin a vintage
at the last moment—or produce wonderful surprises in one
that seemed nothing out of the ordinary!

Chaptalisation or addition of sugar to the must, to assist
fermentation in years when bad weather, low temperatures or
similar hazards make it difficult for the wine yeasts to work as
they should without extra 'fodder', is sometimes permitted, but
it is subject to strict governmental controls. In fine years it is
not necessary and, even when it is, the greatest care must be
taken to avoid the wine being thrown off balance and made too
high in alcohol. The amount of added sugar is therefore kept to
the minimum.

The fermentation begins naturally, within 24 hours or sometimes sooner, and goes on for about 5–7 days. During this time
the grape sugar in the must will decline, being consumed by the
yeasts, and the alcoholic content will rise. The temperature of
the vat is carefully watched: above 32°C it can be
dangerous—in the past, in certain hot years the wines virtually
pasturised themselves in the vat—so that cooling devices of
various kinds now control the process of fermentation
throughout, for if the must temperature rises to more than 35°
the fermentation stops, sugar remains in the wine, and, even if
the process can be started up again, the wine risks being completely ruined.

The new wine remains in the vat for the length of time
required—that is to say, according to the type of wine to be
made; in the past it would stay there for a month or more, the
wine meanwhile absorbing tannin and other elements from the
grapeskins and debris. This makes for long life—but for wines
that can be hard and undrinkable when young. Nowadays it is
seldom economic to make a vintage that won't be even vaguely
palatable for 2–3 years, so the procedure has been adapted to
produce wines that, in general, will be drinkable in light vintages within 3–5 years, in good vintages 8–12, and in great vintages some estates can still—just—manage to make wines that,
in accordance with tradition, can live as long as a man or
longer, though ideally, to satisfy the need for turning over stock
quickly, the wines may now be perfectly drinkable at 10–12
years.

There are many who, without necessarily having much
experience of wines made in the old way (such people would,
now, have to be of an age when the tasting sensibilities of most
laymen would be tending to decline anyway), lament that wines
made according to modern scientific procedures cannot

possibly have the quality of those made in former times, when greater longevity was not merely a possibility but an inevitable and integral part of the making of claret. But it really is not possible to make more than hesitant comments about this. Until very recently, many firms and even greater estates were content to go on making their wines as their ancestors had done. The intricacies of fermentation were not familiar and, when things went wrong or somehow succeeded contrary to expectations, it was put down as part of the 'mystery' of wine.

Wine is certainly a mysterious thing, but so is any form of life. Further understanding of the factors that influence the development of life either benignly or malevolently can enable those responsible to protect a living thing, cure it of any ills it suffers and enhance it in every way: the comparison can be vividly appreciated if you think of the ways in which human beings are produced, cared for and brought up today as against fifty years ago. The same is true as regards wines. Of course some very great and long-lasting wines were made (sometimes more by luck than skill) in the past. But those whose experience in wine is far greater than my own are confident that the subtlety and fascination of present-day wines can equal or surpass those of, say, the beginning of the twentieth century, even if their prime drinking period may not be as long.

MATURATION

The new wine is run off into casks after the fermentation in the vat has finished. It is now 'in wood', and in great vintages new oak is used as much as possible; certain estates that can afford the expense often use new wood for each vintage, but others consider that, in an average year, an old cask—like a matured wooden vat—may have something to give to the wine. However, with some wines the makers may continue the maturation process in another vat or large container of various types. But the wines of the great estates will certainly be matured in wood—that is, in casks.

The 'mash' of grapeskins and debris is then pressed, about the only time when pressing, in the generally understood sense, is carried out. Imagine a large meat press, or weight coming down on a mass of pulp contained in a wooden vessel with space between the side slats, so that the juice can run out. The first pressing, which merely gets the final drops out of the mash, is then also put aside into a cask, but the second and third pressings are kept separate. The result of the first pressing may be added to the *grand vin* or estate wine if this seems to require the additional tanning and general stalkiness that will be in this *vin de presse*. Second and third pressings are reserved for various uses, and may be only used domestically. The squashed mass of what remains of the pressing can be utilised for distillation or fertiliser.

The term *grand vin* has various meanings, according to the context in which it is used. When it relates to the wine that is being made in the *chai*, to which the *vin de presse* may be added (if this particular addition can benefit the wine overall) then the meaning can be translated as 'estate wine'. But this is the only way in which it would be correct to translate the term—or as 'the wine that bears the label or labels of the property'.

However, to refer to a wine in general as a *'grand vin'* has no relevance to the process whereby it was made; nor can it be adequately translated as 'a great wine', any more than *'un vin fin'* may be translated as 'a fine wine'—the significance is simply not the same. A *'grand vin'* in general terms means something relating to the wine's stature, its potential—a wine of breeding, charm, finesse, with aristocratic quality. But when someone making wine is talking about the wine that is being produced to bear the label of the estate, this will be the *'grand vin'*, whether or not it does, eventually, merit being described with any of the adjectives used in the previous sentence. I suppose it might, in the context of wine making, be translated as the 'main or principal wine'.

The casks or *barriques* are distinguished as being Bordeaux *barriques* by the piece of wood across the cask head, each end of which has a serrated edge. The cask rims are of cane, bound with willow at the ends. Or, if they are *barriques de transport* for shipping or (nowadays) long-term storage, they have metal tops and bottoms. They are filled to capacity and the bunghole is therefore on the top (*bond dessus*). The bung itself rests only lightly in the bunghole, so that any additional gases given off in the final stages of fermentation (such as occur when the malic acid of the wine is converted into lactic acid, and also in the secondary fermentation in the spring after the vintage) can easily escape. The process of fermentation can make the wine 'work', bubbling quite violently, so that the gas given off has to be able to escape from the cask. It is important to keep the casks full, so that the air cannot affect their contents while the wine is still 'making itself', and they are topped up every two days.

Every three months or so they are racked; this means that the wine is run off and put into another cask, leaving the lees—the deposit which will have settled in the cask and is then left behind (and is sometimes used to make the everyday wine for the estate staff). During the period February–April after the vintage, the process known as *égalisage* takes place: this means that the contents of the various vattings (the grapes are picked according to variety, and at different times) are combined. The word 'blend' has a stupidly pejorative association in English, but in fact, as all wine is a blend of different vines, different vine varieties, different parts of a vineyard and, for non-vintage wines, different years, it would be quite impossible to make an 'unblended wine' unless this were done from one single vinestock—which would only make about one litre of wine.

The art of the blender is of enormous importance, and the *égalisage* takes place in accordance with the types and ages of vines, the way in which different vattings (*cuvées*) turn out, the weather and the laboratory reports. Each vat is carefully appraised before the process is undertaken, and every single cask is tasted and a report make out. Sometimes a whole vat may be rejected if it is unsatisfactory. The spring rackings, combined with the *égalisage*, are therefore about the first indication of quality; even the owner of an estate may only have a general idea—and hope—about the quality of a vintage (of course, the quantity can be counted) until the next spring. The wines are then racked off into wood.

Up to this time they may indeed have been in wood—that is, in casks—but the casks into which they will have been run off from the vat are those that simply receive the contents of the various vattings as the fermentation of those vats are completed. After the *égalisage*, the blend of the wines that have previously been in wood (casks) then is returned to finish the process of maturation in wood (casks). It should be stressed that, although the wines of the great estates are invariably made in this way, other wines of the region may be returned from the vat to other vats for maturation; there can be advantages for certain types of wine to undergo their final finishing in a large receptacle (a maturation vat) as compared with a small one (a cask). It is also important to realise that a vat in which fermentation takes place may be wood, stainless steel, glass or enamel-lined tanks—but this is not necessarily the type of vat in which maturation may take place. Some wines require and deserve a slow maturation, which they get in wooden casks; others woud not necessarily improve in quality by this form of maturation and are therefore matured in different vessels. But the great estates will use the system of the cask—*barrique*—as I have outlined.

Towards the end of their first year, the wines are 'fined'—that is, the particles that remain in them are attracted by a substance, in this instance egg-white (many great estates have found it essential to use only free-range hens for these eggs)[*] which catches the particles; the fining is put into each cask and, at that time and for a little while after (about 6 weeks or more) the wine is not in a fit state to appraise by tasting.

Then it is again racked off and goes into the second year *chai* or store, above ground (except for certain estates which are so situated that they can have true cellars below ground), while the first year *chai* is prepared for the reception of the new vintage. The wine fills the casks and, now, these are turned so that the

---

[*] All fining matters—others are isinglass and blood—are albuminous. They act by putting an opposite electro-static charge to the solid matter in the wine.

bung is at the side (*bond de côté*) and tightly stoppers the cask. If a sample has to be drawn, instead of inserting the *velenche* or pipette through the bunghole, as in the first year *chai*, a small hole has to be made in the cask head (a process known as spiling the cask) and either a tap is inserted or, more usually,

Using the velenche

the person drawing off the sample will exert pressure on the cask head by levering something against the piece of wood that crosses the head (often a type of claw-headed hammer is used) so that the wine is forced out into the glass for sampling. (If you simply bore a hole in the head of a full cask, the pressure inside is so great that only a slow leak will result, and that after a time; there will be no flow of wine.)

This is what the visitor to a *chai* will see in general. There are estates where the wine remains in a vat until it is to be bottled; there are others where it may go into wood for part of its life and then be returned to the vat for a period. It all depends on the type of wine to be made and the judgment of the owner or his advisers.

THE WINE IN BOTTLE

When the wine is bottled at the estate—as happens with all the finer wines nowadays—it is then cased up and sent either to the cellars of a shipper in Bordeaux or else actually despatched to mature in an export market cellar. Visitors to wine estates are often disappointed because they don't see 'old bottles', but the only stocks of bottled wine kept at an estate will be those reserved for the owner. The great estates keep 'libraries' (*bibliothèques*) of their wines in which examples of each vintage for a century or more are kept, also the larger sizes of bottle, and these can go back for nearly two centuries, as in the famous

bibliothèque at Château Lafite. But otherwise an estate has no
storage space for wines in bottle and wants to sell these as soon
as possible; indeed, bids are received and purchases of wines
made from the time that shippers and merchants get an inkling
of what the vintage is like in the spring. But the wine won't be
shipped until it is either in bottle or nearly ready to be bottled
by whoever buys it. British bottling enjoys a high reputation,
but nowadays the estates making the finer wines prefer not to
risk anything happening to their precious product, and bottle it
on its home ground. There is never enough of the finest wines
in great vintages to supply all the would-be customers so
wastage is an irreparable loss.

Exactly when the wine is bottled is the decision of the owner
and/or his manager and cellarmaster: the finest red wines, in
good years, are generally bottled when they are two years old,
but sometimes they may be a few months older and in light
years a little younger. In the past, they might have been three or
even more years old before being bottled. Variations also occur
because of area—some areas bottle early, others late.

White Wines

They are vintaged and made in the same general way as the red
wines, except that there is, obviously, no point in letting the
grapeskins remain in the fermenting must, because they have
no contribution to make to the wine as regards colour. They
must, indeed, be separated from the skins as quickly as possible
and they are crushed or broken up differently from the grapes
used for red wines. A horizontal press, like a large cylinder
lying on its side, is used; generally, this press contains a number
of loops of chain inside, and, as it revolves, these strip off the
grapes from the skins and break up the pulp. Sometimes (but
more often in other areas than Bordeaux) another type of
horizontal press is used, in which the grapes are squeezed by the
expansion of a rubber bag inside the press, but the revolving
press containing chains is the more usual in the Gironde.

Nowadays a process known as *débourbage* (literally translated
as 'cleansing') is also often used for the dry whites; this involves
putting the fresh grape juice into a stainless steel tank for about
24 hours, together with sulphur dioxide, a chemical that is
much used in all wine making to disinfect and clean wines. This
process of *débourbage* removes all the solids in the wine and
prevents there being any risk of premature oxidation (too much
contact with the air, which makes the wines darken in tone and
become prematurely old).

The dry white wines are then vatted, like the reds, and
proceed to mature, either wholly in a vat for maturation, or else
in wood, again like the reds. When they are fined, isinglass or
oxblood are used, instead of albumen, and although some of
the greater dry whites may remain in wood for up to two years,

Horizontal presses

lesser wines and wines of lighter years may be bottled even as
early as the late spring after their vintage, or when they are
merely a year or eighteen months old. It is necessary that they
should be fresh and still in their vigorous youth when they are
bottled.

THE SWEET WINES

It is possible to make the inexpensive and slightly sweet white
Bordeaux simply by allowing the grapes to become fully ripe
and then simply selecting the sweetest wines and, at the time of
the *égalisage*, putting these aside. But the finer sweet wines are
made differently.

The difference starts with the time and way that they are vintaged. In the regions where they are made, notably the Sauternais, a type of autumn fog can settle over the vineyards and this
results in a certain fungus developing on the skins of the grapes
in humid, stuffy weather. As might be expected, rot of the ordinary type (*pourriture grise*—grey rot) is wholly undesirable in a
vineyard, which is why rain at vintage time is so unwelcome,
but this special fungus (*botrytis cinerea*) is known as 'noble rot'
(*pourriture noble*). Its action does not destroy the grapes,
although it shrivels them, gradually working through each
bunch, so that while some of the ripe grapes are green and
plump, others, attacked by the noble rot, become pinkish-grey,
furry with the fungus, and shrivelled as if contracted from the
inside, like old suede gloves. But the noble rot has absorbed
all the surplus moisture inside each grape it attacks, so that the
juice that remains is a drop or two of concentrate, high in
natural grape sugar (the grape is anyway high in sugar, as
slimmers will know). If you can bring yourself to eat a grape
looking like this, you will be astonished that the furry skin
hardly tastes at all—and the luscious, nectar-like juice inside is
delectable.

It is no use to employ ordinary vintagers to pick grapes in these vineyards, for great experience is needed to know exactly when a grape should be detached from its bunch and it is rare that even small clusters, much less whole bunches can be picked at a time; generally, the regular vintagers of the property have to pass through a vineyard many times, on each occasion picking grape by shrivelled grape, which they cut with a pair of special long-bladed scissors. The vintage therefore takes much longer than elsewhere, although small estates may not risk waiting—and risk losing the whole crop as the result of an early frost—and therefore they will pick ripe and nobly rotten grapes together as late as they dare. But at a great estate, picking will go on for 6–8 weeks, at Château Yquem for nearly three months. The vintagers will usually have to go through the vineyard half a dozen times, but at any one of the great properties they may have to do so ten times. This is why such wines are costly to make, in terms of time and skill.

The nobly rotten grapes do not, at the majority of the great estates making sweet wines, go into a vat at all after being pressed, but the juice is pumped straight into casks, usually of new wood, and the wine develops there, being carefully racked and, in due time, the casks are 'equalised' or blended. Bottling time varies greatly, sometimes an Yquem of a great year may remain in wood for more than three years. But, in essentials, the process of maturation is similar to that of the other wines. For the dryish white wines of such great estates as are better-known for their sweet wines, the grapes are simply picked before the noble rot develops on them. Indeed, the discovery of the effect of the fungus on the resulting wine does not appear to have been made until possibly the beginning or middle of the nineteenth century, although the action of the noble rot has

Pourriture noble

been known in Germany since the eighteenth century and the great sweet Tokays were made in Hungary in the seventeenth.

Vines and Grapes

All the red wines and the majority of the whites are made from a mixture of different grapes, black grapes being used for the reds and white grapes for the whites. Sometimes people query this, supposing the blend of grapes to be somehow less inclined to produce a great wine than a single variety; some American writers on wine actually still promulgate the belief that wines made from one type of vine (or *varietal*) are superior.

As far as the Bordeaux region is concerned, however, it is precisely this combination of certain types of vine that makes the wines of the area so fine and so fascinating. Different vineyards and, indeed, different estates will plant the permitted vines in different proportions, according to what the soil and climate suggest may be most advantageous. The variations in the resulting wines are enormous.

GRAPES USED FOR RED WINE

Cabernet Sauvignon. This is one of the great red wine grapes of the world and gives the nobility, underlying forcefulness and soaring, elegant bouquet to fine claret. To register the Cabernet Sauvignon dominating the other vines in a great red Bordeaux, try to taste one of the fine years of Mouton-Rothschild, as this estate makes particular use of this grape. If you try a wine made in other vineyards throughout the world solely from the Cabernet Sauvignon, you will probably notice its assertive, definite style.

Cabernet Franc. Another name in the Gironde for this grape is Bouchet or Bouchey. This variety of Cabernet gives a light, fresh fruitiness to claret, plus an immediately appealing, albeit slightly obvious fragrance. If you want to sample wines made from the Cabernet Franc alone, try one of the finer red wines of the Loire, such as Chinon or Bourgueil, and note the crispness and delicate fruity flavour.

Merlot. This is the grape that the vintagers pick to slake their thirst, for, unlike most wine grapes, it is rather succulent and fleshy. It gives a wine a close-textured, scented bouquet and rounded style. Too much Merlot can make a vulgar wine, but, to see how great its charm can be, try a Lafite-Rothschild, where the Merlot usually succeeds in twining itself around the two types of Cabernet to make a claret that is enticing and delicious, as well as noble and elegant. Merlot used to be charily used, because of its susceptibility to rot, but new stocks are more resistant.

Malbec. This grape gives a slight velvetiness to wines but, used in too high a proportion, can make a claret common.

Petit Verdot. This grape provides an acidity that can make a

claret crisp and fresh; it also gives a strong clour to the wine.
Carmenère. Less used nowadays, this is a grape that can give
push and body to certain types of clarets.

It will be realised that each of these classic wine grapes has
something to contribute and, too, that each of them may have
certain vulnerable points or weaknesses. The Merlot, for example, is susceptible to both mildew and a disease called *coulure*,
when the grapes remain small and unripe and eventually just
fall from the vine. In some vintages, a vine disease may virtually
destroy a particular type of grape, so that the character of the
wine eventually made may be unexpected and untypical of the
property. Because of the individuality of the vines, too, vin-
taging takes place according to the vine variety and the particular site of the vines, sometimes several days lapsing between
one plot and one type of vine being picked and that when
another variety will be vintaged.

GRAPES USED FOR WHITE WINES

Sauvignon. Nothing to do with the Cabernet Sauvignon, this is
one of the great white wine grapes of the world. It gives the
backbone to the white Bordeaux and, with its distinctive fresh
bouquet and firm, lingering flavour, it usually makes a very
good wine, even if the proportion of Sauvignon in the blend is
small. Many Sauvignons are now made in France in various
regions: when you try one, register the astonishingly assertive
bouquet and what I think of as the 'cold steel' of the flavour.
Sémillon. This is a grape that makes rather fragrant, sometimes
sweet white wines all over the world. It gives the flowery, sweet
bouquet and slight softness—which need not necessarily be
sweet, although it can be—to the white Bordeaux, and it is one
of the grapes that is most important in the vineyards making
the great sweet wines.
Muscadelle. Like all vines belonging to the Muscat family, this
is one of pronounced, languorous bouquet. A little of it goes a
long way, but its opulence can enhance many of the sweet or
sweetish wines.

What the Wines are like

It is difficult to attempt a description of what any wine tastes
like, for taste is a subjective sensation and cannot yet be defined
in rigid terms. True, a French publication does try to measure,
for example, the seconds during which a wine remains on the
palate (the length of the after-taste), or the 'finish'—but many
wouldn't agree with this either! (And why should they?)
Perhaps the best that can be done here is to express as clearly as
possible the kind of impressions a particular wine makes on
me, a fairly experienced drinker but someone who has never
been in the wine trade, and hope that the reader will, at some

stage, find some point of contact, even if this only subsequently involves translating one person's tasting impressions into those of somebody else, or provoking something constructive by way of disagreement. For example, if it's easier for you to sum up a wine in terms of music, or flowers, or types of people, then it's for you to translate into your terms what I mean when I write that a wine is "gentle", "lighthearted", "bouncy", "sinewy"—or whatever.

As regards Bordeaux, no two people will ever agree exactly as to how the finer wines should be described in words, even though sometimes a word or phrase can inspire an individual to make a personal tasting tag—obviously more useful than that of someone else. Trying to describe a taste is rather like trying to interpret a symphony in terms of a water-colour, or to express what someone who plays championship golf or is a star of the dance is like by taking a photograph or writing a sonnet! However, it can help if you evolve your own set of terms.

In one small area, such as that of a *commune* (parish), each single estate may make wines that have no more than a vague resemblance to each other, as witness the wines of Lafite, Latour and Mouton, all first growth Pauillacs, yet each one as different from the others as individual human beings. Of course, differences are increased because of the individual proportions of the grape varieties grown in each vineyard, because of the age of the vines in different plots, because of the various methods of handling the grapes, the detailed conduct of the fermentation and the infinitely variable routines and forms of care with which the wines are matured. Yet, even when vineyards are neighbours and the wine of the two vineyards is made by the same processes and by the same people in the same *cuvier* and matured in the same *chai*—as takes place at Léoville and Langoa Barton—the minute variations of soil and subsoil, alterations in the curves of the landscape that the eye may notice, changes in the angle at which the sun will strike certain rows of vines, and, below ground, differences in the source of the type of water that nourishes the vines, all these dozens, even hundreds of things will make one fine wine essentially different from another that might superficially be expected to be like it. Then there are the differences resulting from micro-climates: hail will destroy one crop yet leave unscathed the vineyard ten or twenty yards away; rain will dampen one section of a vineyard at a critical moment for good or ill, but on the other side of the road the vineyard will remain dry.

However, it is helpful to have certain vineyard characteristics in mind when tasting, as, even if an exception to the general rules is found, there can usually be seen to be some kind of family resemblance. There will be more definite individuality noticeable in the greater wines, but nowadays improved methods of cultivation and wine making have resulted in marked differences becoming obvious in the bourgeois growths as well as the classed growths.

Vintages

The difference made by variations between one year and another can be enormous. Some people do not always find this an attraction. Some years ago there was an attempt on the part of certain estate owners to put out a proportion of their wines as non-vintage château-bottlings because, they said, this guaranteed a certain standard of quality and enabled the wines of indifferent years to be improved by blending them with even a small proportion of the wine of a better vintage. For those who 'drink the label'—in other words, those who care only about the big names and reputations of the wines they buy, rather than honestly considering the quality of the wine itself, this might seem to appeal. (Or for those who only ever want to drink a 'safe', constant, and possibly characterless type of wine anyway.) Fortunately, however, the high price inevitable with producing a wine of this kind and the circumstances of several good and abundant vintages occurring about the time the trend became evident made the whole notion unsuccessful—to the satisfaction of the true claret lover, for whom the variations of the vintages are one of the charms of this great wine. After all, if the wine is unworthy of the estate name, it can—and, in my opinion, should—be used for either the *sous marque* or 'second wine' of the property, or be declassified to a generic or regional wine, and sold either as in the establishment's own blend, or by someone else as a humbler production altogether.

Tiresomely, the regulations that govern declassification at the present time do not always enable the estate or company to declassify when the owners or wine makers have actually been able to judge how good or inferior the wine may be: the decision has to be taken too soon after the vintage for them to give the wine they have made a fair appraisal, so that there are occasions when the wine of an estate really doesn't deserve the label of the property; this label should imply that the contents of the bottle are a true *grand vin*, worthy of maintaining the reputation of the property.

But there are other things to be considered: in one year, perhaps a part of the crop, say one grape variety, may have been affected by rot or disease, so that the resulting wine is either unbalanced or at least not wholly in character as to what might have been expected. In other years, certain grape varieties enjoy such perfect conditions that they may overshadow certain others.

Whether or not you like the result is personal. For example, I admit to not liking the very great years of Mouton-Rothschild, which seem to me to be 'too much of a good thing'—the predominance of Cabernet Sauvignon in the vineyard means that, in years when this grape ripens to perfection, the wine is so big, so overwhelming, so forceful that, in my view, it lacks the charm, restraint, subtlety and nobility that I myself think great claret should have. But the 'off' or 'light' years of Mouton, when this pushing characteristic of the Cabernet Sauvignon is less evident, are glorious wines—to me.

Sometimes, too, even in this scientific age, a wine can surprise everyone and stand out, long-term, in what might have been considered a light vintage. For example, in 1962 Palmer made what (first growths excluded) was considered the outstanding wine of the year: 1962 was a light, charming vintage, but that wine was a great wine, still demonstrating both charm and also nobility twelve years later. The 1962 Lafite, subtler and still slightly compact and reserved, was both delicious and magnificent when fourteen years old—and with a future yet to come!

Sometimes people are suspicious of the statements issued by merchants and shippers that "even in this generally poor vintage, some good wine was made". True, nowadays, it is rare—without a widespread frost or equally widespread hailstorms—that a vintage is a total loss, for even then some drinkable wine can be made whereas, formerly, it might have been sour, watery or not worth making at all. In very bad years a great estate will not put the label of the property on a wine considered unworthy of it—there was no Palmer 1963, for example. But it is fair to say that, when buyers abound and prices rise, it takes great integrity—plus personal forcefulness and courage—for anyone to insist on relegating a wine that might make a profit to a secondary category, or even to reject a section of the vintage when the vattings are appraised.

In a great year, carelessness can still result in an indifferent wine. So, in a poor year, great care and informed skills can make fair to goodish wine if the resources and knowledge are available. But not even the most skilled technician can make a great wine in a poor year—such as 1968—although a fairly agreeable one might be achieved. And nowadays, when economic pressures make it necessary to produce wines that will be drinkable earlier than they might have been before 1961, there are some wines that, early on, are delicious drinks and wholly enjoyable (whereas, in former times, they might have been less pleasant while young but have had a chance of getting to the category of 'great'). By way of compensation, many bourgeois growths are now able to give the drinker all but the greatest experiences of fine claret and it is not unusual for a well-made bourgeois claret from some of the notable estates in a good or great year to surpass certain classed growths; owners of many bourgeois have to 'try harder' and they do, so that exploration of such wines can be both rewarding and not too expensive.

What makes a Great Vintage?

Curiously, not sunshine alone, although this is important. The sun has to shine at the right time: too much and for too long, and the grapes may never plump out, so that the wine may be hard, high in tannin and very slow to 'come round' (as happened in 1948). A little rain to fill out the grapes—ideally at night, at the end of the summer before the vintage—is welcome. It is true, however, that the recent great vintages have been those in which the rainfall has been small when the overall statistics for the year are totted up. But warmth can ripen grapes as well as actual sunshine.

It is said with some truth that 'It takes two years to make a vintage'. The vines need a certain maturation to enable them to give of their best. In the winter, the frost, when it comes at the right time (not in late spring when the vine is about to flower) can clean and disinfect the ground and prepare the vines for their work of production. One good vintage is often followed by another: 1952/3; 1966/7; 1970/1. There are also longer runs: 1947/8/9 (and even, with certain great estates, 1950); 1959/60/1/2.

A little rain, just before the vintage, increases the quantity and may help the quality. During the vintage it is bad: in 1964 the rain stopped the picking in many areas, notably the Médoc, sometimes for as long as ten days. Not only is it difficult to work in a downpour, but the bloom is also washed off the grapes, so that the wine yeasts have little or nothing to work on; the result then was wines that were often flat, even hollowed out, in their middle flavour, or even downright 'watery', except in regions and at estates where the picking started early, before the rain.

This applies to red wines; the Sauternais need a certain amount of moisture to fill out the grapes, but they also need a humidity to produce the 'noble rot'. Consider where their vineyard lie—usually on low ground. The St. Émilion and Pomerol vineyards, on a hillside and with more air around them, usually made good 1964s because the rain, even when it did affect them, didn't soak the grapes so much because of the greater aeration of the sites. Consider also when the vintage may start: obviously the Graves, Premières Côtes and all regions that are south of Bordeaux will have grapes ripened before the vineyards of the Médoc, and the north of the Médoc will vintage later than the south. Some estates will wait until the risk of rain or change in the weather is a definite hazard before they will start picking; others play safer and pick as soon as the grapes are fairly ripe. The result can usually be detected in the wines; in some years those who pick early may benefit (as in the Médoc in 1964) whereas in others, those who delay, even hazardously, can make exceptional wines (as in 1971).

It isn't always the greatest of vintages that gives the most pleasure. The stupid snobbery of wine has cultivated a custom for those who buy 'the vintage' as much as those who 'drink the label'. But you don't always want to drink a very great wine any more than you always wish to eat elaborate food; this should be one that has been carefully prepared and decanted, introduced by at least one lesser wine, and accompanied by selected dishes. Indeed, how can you sincerely want to drink this kind of wine every day or at a casual type of meal? There's the pleasant—and not improbable—tale of the British nanny looking after the infants of a great wine dynasty, who adjured one of the youngsters "No, you can't have your glass of water until you've drunk up your Mouton 1947". The greatest wines are taxing—to the senses, to the intelligence, and, sometimes, to the digestion! No one would want to listen to a symphony, an opera and a great chorale all day and every day. Hence the great wines should be reserved for great occasions, when they can be enjoyed as they deserve.

The good vintages are more accommodating, but they too should be considered as 'something special'. Those who treat them with over-familiarity, drinking them in coarse glasses with totally unsuitable food, are missing the pleasure they can give—and not getting their money's worth.

The wines of light years can be delicious, either to introduce something more important or to partner means that are themselves lighter and more informal. Those of 'off' years that are successful can be most interesting. And, as has already been indicated, they can be important in their own right. The 'off years' of Château Latour, for example, even as far back as the early 1920s, are great delights for those who are able to enjoy them.

Bourgeois growths usually mature more quickly than classed growths, but the borgeois growths that are themselves a bit tough and robust, such as those from St. Estèphe, are likely to be slower to give of their best than those from communes where wines of a more easily enjoyed and, often faster maturing style are made, such as St. Julien, Margaux and St. Émilion.

Notes on recent vintages will be found on pages 45–46. But it may profitably be borne in mind that the wine that a British claret-lover both likes and finds acceptable may not be the wine that even a good wine waiter in Bordeaux will recommend. For example, one of the best *sommeliers* in the region demurred at serving a member of the wine trade and myself a particular St. Émilion: "Because it is not what customers will expect of a St. Émilion". The wine was one that my host knew and therefore insisted on having, an excellent and well-balanced claret, but—and the wine waiter was quite right—without the slight earthiness and four-square style that many drinkers, ordering a St. Émilion, might expect.

It is dangerous to generalise here, but I think that many ordinary French drinkers of claret like the more obvious wines, the estates that go in for making wines with pronounced, assertive bouquet and smoothish, fairly lingering style. The British drinker, except for the more informed and experienced, may opt for the clarets that have what is sometimes (to the regret of those such as myself) described as 'bite' (which no claret should have, anyway!). These are the wines with great concentration, a 'woofy' smell, lacking subtlety but pronounced in attack, with a certain fat, almost cooked flavour and, possibly, a lack of follow-on. There is, naturally, no reason why wines of both these types should not give both sorts of drinker pleasure—but they are neither or them 'claret', as those who make the finer wines, buy and sell them, and love drinking them as works of the wine maker's art, understand the word.

General Characteristics of Vintages of Red Bordeaux

1950: A light, agreeable year, though by now all but the greatest wines will be thin and showing their age.

1951: An off year. Few wines bearing this date will now be available.

1952: This is a vintage much under discussion by those who still have any of the wines! In the Médoc the wines tended to remain hard, elsewhere they can sometimes now show a certain nobility—but they may be still 'asleep' for a long time to come. The next vintage overshadowed them.

1953: Very charming wines were made, many with nobility and finesse. Some are now beginning to go downhill.

1954: An off-vintage, although some pleasant short-lived wines were made. Now they will probably be well past their prime.

1955: This vintage was not very agreeable at the outset, although some wines showed definite and aristocratic style. Now the finer ones are beginning to display more quality, but they are obviously hard to come by.

1956: This vintage came after the terrible spring frosts. The St. Émilion and Pomerol vines were severely damaged, and elsewhere the wines tended to be acid and thin.

1957: These wines promised somewhat indifferent at the outset, but only small quantities were made. Today they can be very pleasing. There are virtually no St. Émilion/Pomerol wines bearing this date at all. In general a good, perhaps not fine vintage.

1958: Another off-vintage, with few wines of any quality at all. Unlikely to be listed now.

1959: A vintage of both quantity and quality. Some are now beginning to get a little old, except for the greatest, but these wines had charm and grace, the red Graves being really fine and many Médocs of true magnificence.

1960: A year usually described as "light", but some very pleasant

wines, balanced and true to their types were made. The greater
estates made delicious wines.

1961: A very great vintage indeed. The wines seem never to have
gone through a period of sulkiness or dumbness, always being
temptingly drinkable, as regards charm, nobility and extraor-
dinary depth. Many have been drunk—but I am among those who
think they haven't yet come to their prime.

1962: Very pretty clarets, classic albeit small-scale, now beginning to decline except for the greater estate wines.

1963: An off year. A lot of red Graves was made, but in general this
is not a vintage on which to take a chance anywhere.

1964: The heavy rain during the vintage made these wines very
variable. The red Graves, picked slightly earlier, can be very fine
indeed, certain St. Émilions and Pomerols are also extremely
good, fruity and robust wines. In the Médoc there were enormous
variations between estates even in the same commune because so
much depended on the date of picking. The good wines are beginning to show a unified, fair-sized character.

1965: Rain spoiled the vintage. Such estates as did put their labels
on the bottles made wines that are virtually rosés.

1966: A very fine vintage, still not ready, wines with fruit, depth
and on-coming style.

1967: A lighter vintage, with many extremely pleasant, easy to like
wines, some of which are now beginning to get a little old and
tired.

1968: A generally poor year.

1969: Robust wines, rather lacking in charm and delicacy. A good
vintage to choose from a restaurant list, because the wines come
forward quickly, but there are few with any finesse.

1970: A fine vintage and a lot of wines made, that are still
developing and will do for many years. True quality.

1971: A lighter vintage, but the grace and appeal of the wines,
many of which can already be enjoyed, should not mislead
drinkers into thinking that they will not last—some of the estates
made wines that are thought to be even finer than the 1970s. The
red Graves are especially good and so are such Médoc estates as
usually make wines notable for their charm and elegance.

1972: A lightish year, the wines appearing rather mean and dull,
some being somewhat acidic.

1973: This was a light vintage, but those who knew how to make
the wines cleverly have produced some pretty, appealing wines,
some ready for drinking, all likely to have short lives.

1974: Generally coarse in style, lacking grace or charm.

1975: A very fine, in some instances great vintage, which needs
keeping for many years yet.

1976: Rain at vintage time made this a very varied year. Some
wines are too light, sharp and weak, others are adequately pleasant, but will have short lives.

What Claret should give the Drinker

A lot of words (and indeed much purple prose) have been expended on trying to convey the pleasure that claret can give. It is, of course, necessary to apply the usual standards of appraisal to this, as to any other wine, and the section on Tasting may be referred to (pages 96–105). But, by limiting the tasting experience to the red wines of Bordeaux, it is possible to indicate a few more specific characteristics. I cannot do better than to quote what was written about claret by the late Allan Sichel (who, incidentally, taught me most of what I know about wine), shipper and part owner of Château Palmer, owner of Château d'Angludet, of whom even the chauvinistic French admitted that he spoke "with the voice of the vine". This is what he wrote in *An Introduction to Wine* (published by Chambers) in 1952: "Claret is often looked upon as a feminine wine. It has been called the Queen of Wines, as opposed to the Burgundy King, and in this sense it is perhaps the more feminine. If it is a masculine characteristic of wine that it should test the powers of resistance of the body to alcohol, then again claret is a feminine wine. Without being by any means the least alcoholic of wines, it is, possibly, the least heady. If it is a feminine characteristic to whisper rather than to shout, to be subtle in expression rather than blatant, to reject with age the pleasant flamboyant characteristics of youth in favour of the more tranquil, deeper, more expressive qualities of maturity, then again claret is a feminine wine.

"Claret is a kindly, sensitive, proud wine. It will be charming to all who wish to make its acquaintance. It will reveal its innermost self only where confidence will be appreciated and respected. Claret, in short, is capable of expressing beauty and truth; it can delight the palate and nurture the mind of the philosopher in all of us. It is food to the mind, not a bludgeon. It reveals its secret slowly, and becomes at once an inspiration to the striving and a recompense to the successful."

My own postscript to this is that claret is a cerebral rather than a sensual wine—even though certain clarets may be very sensual. If you care for wine at all in addition to finding it an enjoyable drink (the prime purposes of all wine) then you will want to think, even for a few moments, about the claret you drink—and it will make you do so. It will also provide more than immediate pleasure; for, when a great claret is served, the memory of what it was like will not fade merely with that of the meal and the occasion. (I must admit that I have remembered the clarets when I have totally forgotten the circumstances in which they were served or the hosts who provided them—who, on hearing of my forgetfulness, were content to know that the priorities were right!) Also, a pleasant or good claret will make a meal 'to ask a man to', or, for that matter, anyone, even if the fare is simple to the point of bread, butter and cheese. Of course, a great claret deserves something fine by way of accompaniment, but the food should always be on the simple side—which is why many of the traditional British dishes are ideal with the great red wines of Bordeaux. What, then, should claret give to the drinker?

First, its colour.

This can vary greatly, from the darkest purple-plum in fine young wines, to the beautiful tawny-red, verging on orange (*tuilé*, the word which describes the colour of the curved roof-tiles of the south of France, is often used) of the finest old wines. Between these two extremes there is a whole scale of tones, from the 'heart of a rose' crimson to the luminous sheen that, to me, is associated with old silk velvet Coronation robes—in other words, from deep dark red to tawny. Note the shading down of the tones as you tilt the glass—the finer the wine, the more numerous the definite notes in the scale of colours—the 'eye', or centre point of the wine in the glass, may be almost black, the point at which the wine meets the glass pale blue-pink.

Then the smell.

This should never be just a smell. It should be a fragrance, even in the simplest and cheapest Bordeaux, luring the drinker on to taste the wine. In a fine claret the smell can be so subtle, so complex, so enticing that it is not unusual for the comment to be made "Its nose is so beautiful there's almost no need to drink it." But note the "almost". Every claret-lover will be compelled to drink—even if the taste doesn't fulfil the promise of the bouquet. The smell should display the initial charm of claret, whether the wine is a young one, still not really ready to be drunk (but of which the taster makes a note, so as to try it again in several years time), or a wine fully mature, even old, so that the bouquet is delicate and, sometimes, fleeting. Think of the grapes involved (try to pick out the one that 'talks' most immediately) and think of the vintage: does the wine smell profound, or slightly unripe? Does it 'smile' with the assurance of its nobility, or does it appeal, more humbly? Does it cuddle up to the senses of the drinker, or does it stay a little aloof, almost challenging a further exploration? These impressions, gained from the smell, can be linked with the year.

Then, as you taste claret, is the wine soothing, insiduously tempting to tempt the drinker to take another glass? Or does it maintain a certain astringency (which can mean the tannin content is high, implying a possible long future life)? Does it freshen and satisfy, and end cleanly (as do many inexpensive and simple generic wines), or does it linger, tantalising the palate to define what it is really like? Crudely, one might say: do you find the wine sharp, bitter, hard—and not encouraging you to drink more? Or do you sense something in even the least gracious mouthful that makes you suppose that (maybe) there is something that, with time or clever handling, may yield a memorable glass? Young claret can be as gawky as a young person. Certain vaunted estates—and vintages—can be as suave as a type of salesman—and the end result as unpredictable. But sometimes even a 'little' claret will suddenly show the doubtful drinker 'what all the fuss is about'. And a great claret, even if you find you don't really like it or enjoy drinking it, can show off the infinity of colour, smell, flavour, and the 'something extra' that can make a lasting impression.

Don't forget the after-taste: this can indicate the potential of the wine if it is still young, and give enormous pleasure if you savour a matured claret. Breathe downwards after you have swallowed it and then see what sort of impression the wine leaves your sense of smell as well as on your palate.

The Different Regions' Wines

Admitting that certain estates have their individuality and that, in certain vintages, there can be surprises, here are some guidelines to assist identifying the types of wines made in the different areas of the Gironde.

Bourg and Blaye. Both red and white wines are made in both regions, Bourg making more red than white, and Blaye slightly more white than red. The white wines, which can include sweetish wines, are seldom seen labelled as such outside their region, but can be pleasant lightish drinks.

The red Bourgs have a slightly earthy, gutsy style and compact, definite bouquet that the British public usually likes very much. In the past they were famous; indeed, up to the seventeenth century, they would sell at higher prices than the Médocs.

Blaye reds tend to be somewhat lighter, open-textured and sometimes seem rather coarser than those of Bourg, but they too can make agreeable clarets on a small scale.

Cubzac. Around St. André de Cubzac both red and white wines are made, the reds being fairly full-bodied, the whites light and dryish.

Fronsac (including Côtes de Canon Fronsac and Côtes de Fronsac). Both red and white wines are made, but it is the reds that are the most interesting, lightish but with a definite and elegant bouquet and trim style. They are very popular in Belgium and The Netherlands, but some come to Great Britain. They are usually excellent value and easy to enjoy.

Côtes de Castillon. Both red and white wines are made, but the reds are the ones most often noted on lists outside the area. They can be good, light little clarets, the very hard limestone of the subsoil (in former times used for building) giving them a crispness and elegance.

Pomerol. Red wines, which have a distinctively different character from those of neighbouring St. Émilion. The vineyard is on a slightly elevated site, with slopes that are important as far as the vines are concerned, but which are almost imperceptible to the eye. The soil is mostly clay, gravel and sand but, most important, in the subsoil there are certain streaks of gravel that give a lightness and elegance to the wines sited here, and there is also a fair amount of ironstone, which endows the wines with great amplitude. In certain years, the wines fromsome of the great Pomerol estates may even be mistaken for Burgundy, because of their finesse and delicacy, combined with a graciousness and sweet, flowing style. They are very amiable: as far as the finer wines are concerned I have sometimes mistaken them for Pauillacs of a fine (not great) year, or, more often, with the gentle, aristocratic red Graves.

Pomerol has made fine wine since Roman times. The Knights of St. John of Jerusalem had a 'commanderie' in the area during the twelfth century. The wine producers are proud of their traditions and, although the wines have not been classified, it is fair to say that it is rare to find a Pomerol that is not a delight to the informed lover of claret. The areas of Néac and Lalande de Pomerol are part of this vineyard, and Libourne, Côtes de Castillon, and Côtes de Francs may also be considered, essentially, as Pomerols.

St. Émilion. This large vineyard comprises many divisions: St. Émilion Côtes (slopes), St. Émilion Graves (predominantly gravelly), and the following, with the place name attached: Sables, Lussac, Montagne, Saint-Georges, Puisseguin, Parsac. The vineyard is made up of a series of slopes with varying aspects, alongside the town of St. Émilion itself and beyond. The differences of soil and subsoil are considerable, but it is of interest to note that, in the latter, there can be traces of prehistoric shellfish, which are of value to certain crops, including vines.

St Émilion

According to the altitude, aspect and type of estate, the wines naturally vary a great deal, but in general tend to possess a warmth and weight that makes them very much liked by northern export markets; to me they usually have an earthy, ironstone flavour, with a meatiness to the big wines. Because of the situation of the vineyard, a vintage that is elsewhere rather unsuccessful may triumph in St. Émilion, although there are only a few properties that, for quality, can rank with the greater Médocs and Graves. These are robust rather than subtle wines, gorgeous shire horses rather than bloodstock, and they give much pleasure. They are sometimes referred to as 'the Burgundies of Bordeaux'.

The St. Émilion vineyard itself is very old. The fourth-century poet Ausonius is supposed to have had his villa Lucaniac where Château Ausone now commemorates him. The traces of the lines of stone between which the Romans planted their vines can still be seen just outside the walls of St. Émilion. The governing body of the area, the Jurade of St. Émilion, was given its Charter by King John of England in 1199, and the Jurade today is one of the most active in publicising and protecting the quality of the local wines.

Entre-Deux-Mers. This huge area gets its name because of being situated between the two 'seas', the Rivers Dordogne and Garonne. There are many sub-divisions, and both red and white wines are made, but it is the whites that are the most important: the vines planted today are, increasingly, the Sauvignon, to cater for the demand for dry whites. The region is very varied—and very attractive—and the amounts of sand, silex and limestone are propitious to the production of good dry white wines. In former times sweet and very sweet whites were also made here. The whites today are beginning to acquire a new reputation for quality, and can be lightly fresh and crisp, with a faintly flowery bouquet. They tend to be 'small-scale' wines but—and this also applies to the reds—they can give great enjoyment for summer and informal drinking.

Graves de Vayres. This is an area between Bordeaux and Libourne, where the terrain produces wines of individual style because of the sand, gravel and chalk of the topsoil in many places in conjunction with clay, and a predominance of gravel and some sand in the subsoil. Red and white wines are made, the whites moderately full-bodied and quite fresh, the reds—which are likely to be more important—possessing a marked delicacy and crisp stylishness. They are 'smallish-scale' wines for people who don't like 'obvious' clarets, and they can give great pleasure.

Premières Côtes de Bordeaux. This vineyard extends along the east bank of the Garonne from Carbon Blanc, north of the river from Bordeaux itself, southwards to just beyond St. Macaire. There are two sub-divisions, Gabarnac and Cadillac, and many villages that give their names to the wines, notably that of Quinsac, where much pink wine is made, and Langoiran, which is specially proud of its whites. Both red and white wines are made, and some of the whites can be sweetish. The chalk and limestone cliffs along the river banks make the area an obvious one for the production of wines with a definite, lively bouquet and a 'small-scale' but elegant style.

Côtes de Bordeaux Saint Macaire. This area, little known in export markets, lies south of the Entre-Deux-Mers and almost at the limits of the Bordeaux vineyard in general. It makes white wines, usually slightly or definitely sweet, and some red, which may bear the names of any of the ten parishes of the region. Possibly the most famous estate is that of Malromé, between St. André du Bois and Verdelais; this property, built in the twelfth century by the Counts of Béarn, was bought in the nineteenth century by Countess Adèle de Toulouse-Lautrec-Monja, where she hoped that her son, the famous painter, might recover his health after his life in Paris. It was here that Toulouse-Lautrec died in 1901, and his grave and memorial are in the churchyard at Verdelais. It is also at Verdelais that the great man of letters, François Mauriac, lived at his family property of Malagar, which also makes wine.

Graves. The great vineyard extends from the suburbs of Bordeaux itself to beyond Léognan in the south, and, to the west, up to the vast pine forests of the Landes. It is one of the oldest vineyards of Bordeaux, and within it are contained the regions of Cérons and Sauternes. Both red and white wines are made, sometimes a single estate making the two types of wine. The soil, as may be inferred from the place name, is essentially gravelly and stony, including elements of silex and sand, or clay; there are streaks in the subsoil of ironstone, clay and limestone. It is an area suited to the production of very fine wines, although perhaps the great Graves are not always easy for the beginner in wine to understand: the whites are dry, or faintly sweet but not luscious, with a smiling, amiable softness even when they possess a firm, dry flavour and crisp finish. Those from the greater estates can age with great charm, but the taste for them is somewhat particular, and their qualities are not always immediately evident, especially to the drinker who is convinced that he or she has a predominating preference only for wines that are palate-scrapingly dry.

White Graves possess a subtle, almost aromatic bouquet and a lingering flavour that can be wholly beguiling. The red wines can be magnificent, though they too are seldom obvious: their bouquet has often been described as 'spicey'; my own tasting notes often use the expresson "*tabac*", referring to the scent of tobacco flowers at dusk that I find enticing in the fine reds. They can be big wines, although they should never be **aggressive** or obvious; it is their subtlety and graciousness that gives them fascination for the lover of fine, delicate claret, and the greatest are equal to the finest Médocs.

Cérons. White wines, dryish or slightly sweet are made in this vineyard. They possess great intensity of bouquet, plus a marked freshness, and can be delightful drinks for occasions when a very sweet wine could be overwhelming. They usually remind me of the sweet but definitely fresh smell of lemon blossom.

Sainte-Croix-du-Mont. Although some red wine is made in this vineyard, it is the whites that are best known, as might be expected from the stony, gravelly soil, and frequent outcrops of limestone rocks. The white wines are definitely sweet, 'small-scale' luscious drinks that should never be cloying. They have been described as miniature versions of Sauternes, which to me seems a fair comment. The Château de Tastes, which dates at least from 1230, changed hands several times in the wars between England and France, and was exempted from taxes from Edward III because of the quality of its wines. Henry IV of England took over the property when the owner died, and gave it to the City of Bordeaux in 1444, in gratitude for the loyalty of the citizens to the English crown.

Loupiac. Red and white wines are made here, but again the whites, which are sweetish, are the best known. They have a marked intensity and aroma, and it is said that they are rather like small-scale Barsacs, because of their odd, almost crisp finish.

Sauternes and Barsac. In fact, Barsac is a separate A.C. and therefore could be considered apart, but it is the five parishes—Sauternes, Barsac, Bommes, Fargues and Preignac—that make up the whole region, so it can be described with them. This is a low-lying, hidden region: the estates are concealed in the vegetation and woods, and the vineyards are enormously varied, according to their altitude, aspect and how they are broken up by the little ridges and valleys. Cocks & Feret* differentiate the soil as: silex and chalk (Barsac), with varying subsoils: more chalk under Barsac, chalk or clay at Bommes, Sauternes and Preignac, and *aliotique* at Fargues. This last descriptive word is local to the south-west of France and very difficult to find in reference books, but the Library of the Institute of Geological Sciences in London kindly tracked it down for me. It refers to "Alios, or a rough sandstone of a dark brown colour". It is this kind of variation in the subsoil that can make such a difference to the wine.

Only white wines are made in Sauternes and Barsac. The dry wines, which cannot be termed "Sauternes" because the

* Called the 'Bible of Bordeaux', the first edition of this book appeared in France in 1850. It lists all the properties of the wine area, and includes comments on the wines, the regulations governing them, and tells what they should be like. The last edition appeared in 1969.

Appelation Controlée defines them as sweet wines (see pages 113–115), are extremely fragrant, rounded and full, lingering along the palate and finishing with an inner firmness and intensity that indicates their stature. Some give the impression by their bouquet that they are going to be sweet.

The sweet wines, made with the *pourriture noble* (pages 36) vary considerably, but it may be helpful to bear in mind that Sauternes in general begin by being perfumed and infinitely luscious, the evocation of ripe fruit and hot sun captured in their flavour, and they end as sweet as they started. The Barsacs, however, usually have a slightly more intense, compact fragrance, an almost subtle sweetness—and they finish with an odd flick of dryness that is deliciously freshening to the palate. Each estate possesses its own special character.

The Médoc. This not markedly prepossessing tongue of land that licks up from Bordeaux along the Gironde estuary to the Atlantic is slightly undulating and parts of it are forested. In no way spectacular, the landscape is often very pleasant, some of the estates have imposing and even beautiful houses. But it is the vineyards that dominate the region all along the east bank of the river and for some distance inland.

The Médoc is usually divided into the Haut-Médoc, which extends from La Jalle de Blanquefort to Saint-Seurin-de-Cadourne, and the Médoc, which is the region from St. Germain d'Esteuil up to Talais and Soulac. Each parish will make wines of individuality, but not every parish has an A.C., so that the overall A.C.s 'Haut-Médoc' and 'Médoc' may apply to wines made in areas distant from each other and differing widely (see pages 113–115). It would take too much space to describe each group of wines, so I shall limit this section to the regions of the specific A.C.s, and to the classed growths and more important bourgeois that will simply be labelled 'Haut-Médoc' or 'Médoc'.

By far the greater part of the wines and all the fine wines of the area are red, although some properties still make a little white wine, often reserving it for the use of the establishment or featuring it as a curiosity on the list of a few specialist merchants or restaurants. The wines made in the *palus* or river-bank plots, although often pleasant, are not included here for reasons of space; the wines from the islands in the estuary are categorised as Bourg or Blaye, except for that made in l'Ile Margaux, which is a Médoc.

Ludon. This parish, with its gravelly, sandy soil, and subsoil that is sometimes gravel and alios, or sand and clay, produces fine, subtle wines, with a delicacy and refinement, plus a wonderful smell, that is typified by the great classed growth, La Lagune.

Macau. This too is gravelly and sandy, with some subsoils of gravel and alios. The classed growth here is Cantemerle, an estate that makes wines of nobility and subtlety, demonstrating the style of Macau, which is a little more austere than Ludon—where the wines are deliciously fruity and amiable albeit compact and aristocratic; Macau wines possess finesse and elegance, Ludon charm. I have mentioned the two classed growths simply because they show the characteristics of their regions in their impeccable wines.

Margaux and Cantenac. The soil of these two parishes tends to be stone and gravel, with greatly varied subsoils, which account for the wide range of wines. The traveller will note the differences in the appearance of vineyards on the river side of the road that runs between many famous properties. The slopes are another factor accounting for the enormous differences in even adjacent estates, and the little *croupes* or ridges, which are often not noticeable to the eye, accentuate these differences.

The wines are gracious, smiling clarets; even in the years when they are light, they usually possess plenty of charm, and, in good years, they have a wonderful warmth and aroma that my notes often interpret as "mulberries" (or "loganberries") "in a walled garden in high summer". They are usually most appealing and delicious clarets with which to begin learning about fine wines. Arsac, Soussans, Labarde, Arcins and Avensan are nearby wine villages of which the wines may be said to bear a type of family resemblance to those of Margaux, even though they are, especially in the classed growths, highly individual.

Moulis. The terrain is diverse: partly sand and gravel, or clay, gravel and marl, and, in certain areas, there is some chalk and clay or gravel and clay. The sub-soils vary likewise, and here too fossilised shellfish have been found in the limestone. It is the lightness, delicacy and close-textured bouquet that make the Moulis wines, in their great variety, appealing to the claret lover who likes a certain elegance and freshness. They can be excellent choices in hot weather and the fact that they are not very well known makes them still good value.

Listrac. Sometimes these wines are considered similar to those of Moulis, but they are not in general as fine. The vineyard is variegated, and some parts quite elevated. The topsoil is mostly gravelly on the little slopes and plateaux, but there is also clay, limestone and marl. The subsoils are inclined to be alios towards the river, gravel, marl and a little limestone elsewhere. The wines are moderately robust in style, a little more open in texture than those of Moulis. They seldom attain the finesse of the latter, but they can be very successful in years when wines from the surrounding area tend to be a little thin and pinched. They are immediately appealing. albeit on a smallish scale.

Lamarque and Cussac. These neighbouring regions make pleasant, definitely fragrant and slightly full-bodied wines on their sandy, gravelly soil, with subsoils of sand and alios in the west, some gravel in the centre, and the rest clay. The Château de Lamarque, built in the fourteenth century, is on the site of much older buildings, and was used by the King of England at one time, and, after the French reoccupied Aquitaine, was frequently the seat of the governor of the province.

Saint-Laurent. This parish is at the beginning of the other great wine regions of the Médoc, as you go north from Bordeaux, and the terrain is extremely diverse, but includes the stony, sandy and sometimes silicaceous soil favourable to fine wine production, with a certain amount of ironstone, as well as clay and limestone in the subsoil. The wines show the beginning of the refined style that is so marked in the next main vineyard. La Tour Carnet, a medieval castle, at one time belonged to the brother-in-law of Michel de Montaigne* who, with his great friend, La Boétie, visited it on several occasions.

Saint-Julien. Slightly undulating vineyards of the pale, stony colour associated with fine wine, and patches of alios, gravel, clay and marl in the subsoil, make this area one of the most agreeable of the 'greats' of the Médoc. There are many great estates, each one as individual as a human being, but all to a greater or lesser extent display the delectable St. Julien style: a close-packed, soft bouquet, a velvety, lengthy flavour and great charm. These are the wines that the beginner can easily like and the experienced appreciate in detail. Some of them have great profundity and a lasting sweetness that is special to this vineyard; as it borders on Pauillac, some of the wines can also possess an extra nobility and firm style. Cocks & Feret (see footnote on page 53) describe St. Juliens as being almost halfway between the wines of Margaux and those of Pauillac; to me, they have a fresh but delicately scented smell, like violets, and a silky texture. At one time the various estates that are now Léoville-Poyferré, Léoville-Lascases, and Léoville and Langoa Barton were all one property, but each one of the wines is distinct from the others today.

Pauillac. This, too, is an undulating vineyard, with some quite steep slopes down to the river and above the town of Pauillac.† The topsoil is invariably stony; underneath it, there is a deep streak of alios. It must be this curious type of sandstone that gives the wines of Pauillac their astonishing quality: long-lived, they are the great nobility of the Médoc, sometimes reserved and almost harsh and edgy when young, they develop a huge bouquet as they age. Some people say this reminds them of the *goût de capsule*, the metallic cover put over the cork, but I have never been able to recognise this. What they do often smell of,

---

* Michel Eyquem de Montaigne (1533–92), at one time Mayor of Bordeaux, but best known for his *Essais*—studies of himself and topics that interested him, of outstanding merit and charm.

† "The vine likes to see the river" is a Médoc saying. A view of it is, indeed, possible from many of the great estates.

to me, is the cedarwood that lines a box of cigars—an aroma verging on the spicey, fresh, but warm and alluring. Their full-bodied, definite and almost overwhelming flavour exemplifies clarets of great breeding, sensitivity and depth of taste, and the way they linger on the palate and, even more so sometimes in the mind, can be a revelation to anyone who has perhaps previously considered claret simply an enjoyable drink.

The finer Pauillacs are not wines to handle casually or serve in haste, they merit time and attention. If you have not yet got to know them, try if possible to arrange that your first experience of drinking them is in the company of somebody who knows a little more, someone who can select a wine that will please as well as impress, and who may be able to tell you something about the multitude of taste impressions it may provide. It is, of course, not reasonable to expect that the smaller-scale classed growths and bourgeois Pauillacs should be capable of attaining the heights of the first growths and finer classified growths, but in general 'nobility' is the overall characteristic of Pauillac wines.

Saint-Sauveur, Cissac, Vertheuil. A number of pleasant, not perhaps well-known wines are made in what is the hinterland of Pauillac. Many of them nowadays can be highly satisfying small-scale clarets, often distinguished by a particularly fine colour and crisp, refreshing flavour.

St. Estèphe. The ground rises beyond Pauillac and the St. Estèphe wines seem to indicate this by their slightly assertive, sometimes stalky and often austere style. There are a number of little hills and ridges, and the ground is quite light in colour and gravelly, with a certain amount of alios in the subsoil. I do not agree with Cocks & Feret in saying that the wines of this parish tend to be "lighter" than those of Pauillac and that they come to maturity rather sooner; in their youth, the St. Estèphes can be hard and definitely reserved, even ungracious, and frequently this phase seems to endure beyond the time when the Pauillacs are softening and becoming welcoming to the drinker. They are not, in my view, wines for the beginner, as their definite character is uncompromising: if you don't like them, you really dislike them. But they can be beautiful wines when they mature, providing a complex, fascinating bouquet, true delicacy of flavour and great length. The bourgeois growths, which are not in danger of being so aggressive when they are young, are often excellent drinking.

Saint-Seurin-de-Cadourne, St. Germain d'Esteuil, St. Yzans, St. Christoly and Bégadan. These are a few of the wine parishes at the top of the Médoc, from whence many good, even fine (albeit small-scale) wines can come. The landscape is varied, forests, crops and market gardens occupying space as well as the vineyards, and there are more distinctive hills and valleys. Obviously it is not possible to generalise about the wines, but they are worth trying on the spot, and those that do feature on export lists are likely to be selected as pleasing to British tastes for their robust style and fresh fragrance.

4

Classification – Crus Classés

The term '*crus classés*' or 'classed growths' will crop up in any discussion of Bordeaux wines. It refers, in general, to the grouping of the wines or growths (*crus*) of the various regions into 'classes', several different sections within each classification. But the most important classification, the one likely to be referred to as 'the classification' without further description, is the classification of 1855, which concerned certain of the red wines of the Médoc and one red Graves. Some understanding of the significance of this and other classifications is necessary, because otherwise visitors risk supposing that a wine which bears the term "*Grand cru classé*" on its label is, just because of this, somehow superior, and that a wine categorised in the Médoc classification as a "third classed growth" is somehow lesser as regards quality than one that is a "second classed growth".

The wines of Bordeaux were 'classified' or grouped in categories from at least the middle of the eighteenth century. But they were grouped according to the prices they were expected to fetch when sold—something that might, but need not be, coincidental with their quality. Certain estates had, by the end of that century, begun to be known far beyond their own region, and the wines of particular parishes or general areas were beginning to be considered as specifically marketable under their commune names. As early as 1824 it was recorded that the English were the biggest buyers of Latour, that nearly all Lafite was drunk in England and that the English market tended to buy all the "first growths (premiers crus) of Pauillac".

In 1855, the Syndicate of Brokers of Bordeaux, whose findings were endorsed by the Bordeaux Chamber of Commerce, made another classification for the Universal Exhibition in Paris in that year. For this, they considered the white wines of Sauternes and Barsac separately, and made another classification of over 60 red wines from the Médoc, plus Haut Brion from the Graves. It is this classification of the red wines that is 'the' classification—although, to avoid confusion, the qualifying phrase "of 1855" should be added. It must be stressed that the selection of the brokers of the wines then available, and the order in which they put them, was only their judgment at the time—and it related to the prices that the wines might fetch. For example, some estates had been broken up at the time of the Revolution and therefore were not even considered in 1855; one very fine growth was actually in the hands of receivers in 1855, so it was placed rather low, another estate now famous for its impeccable wines had only recently begun to be sold on the Bordeaux market so was put low also; and the brokers did not even taste all the wines. However, this particular classification still stands as in 1855, although some estates mentioned have virtually stopped producing, their names having virtually disappeared; and some have declined considerably in reputation. In recent years, Baron Philippe, owner of Mouton-Rothschild, campaigned incessantly until, in 1973, Mouton was raised to the ranks of the first growths, where its owner's opinion thought it should always have been and, indeed, the price its wines have commanded would entitle it to be. But this has been the only major change.

There are frequent attempts at a reclassification both by official bodies and individuals, notably the suggestion of Alexis Lichine, whose preoccupation with the matter somewhat distorts his otherwise excellent encyclopaedia.* Obviously, owners whose estates might be relegated to lower places—however little this really signifies in terms of quality—have been resolutely opposed to any change, and the possibility of admitting some properties from the ranks of the bourgeois growths complicates the matter.

It is probably fair to say that the classed growths of the Médoc should all be and usually are fine wines. It is unfair to imply that certain third, fourth and fifth growths are generally in any way inferior to second growths or even, in some years, to certain first growths—this naturally varying according to the vintage. All have their reputations to maintain. The first growths are undeniable aristocrats, but they, too, inevitably vary over the years and from year to year. One of them went through a period within living memory of making wines that most authorities considered to be unworthy of the estate at its finest.

The first growths established the firm tradition of only château-bottling their wines some years after World War II; they also offer their wines on the Bordeaux market rather later than the other growths, thereby giving some indication of the level at which prices may be expected to be for that particular vintage. Publicity for their wines, notably in the United States,

* *Encyclopaedia of Wines & Spirits* (Cassell).

has resulted in prices remaining high and, because supplies are necessarily limited, the owners and the companies who direct the estates take care to ensure that stocks are shared between world markets and reputable retail outlets.

There is a tendency towards national preferences for some wines, also fashions for certain estates; this may be because of real or supposed associations with a property with a name that doesn't sound French, or with one that is owned by a family with origins or connections outside France. Or it may simply be that certain properties make wines that appeal specifically to certain export markets. The reputation of any classed growth is carefully maintained and, nowadays, this tradition extends to many other properties that were classed prior to but not included in the 1855 classification, and of course also includes all the other growths that have been classified in more recent times. It is worth noting that it is not obligatory for an estate to indicate its specific classification on its label; this is up to the individual estate policy. For example, Lafite never has, but Latour does.

In 1953 the red Graves were classified, in 1955 St. Emilion, and in 1959 the white Graves; the conditions in which these classifications were made were in no way similar to those of 1855, and therefore it is wrong to make direct comparisons as regards quality between the different classed growths of different areas. These later classifications were made by the Syndicats de Défense des Appellations Graves et St. Émilion, and l'Institut National des Appellations d'Origine, working with the Ministry of Agriculture.

In 1932 and again in 1966 the bourgeois growths (*crus*) of the Médoc were classified, but the second classification was very different from the first, due to the many changes that had taken place during the intervening years. Space does not permit all the names of the bourgeois *crus classés* to be given, but, in 1932, there were six rated as '*Crus exceptionnels*', 97 as '*Bourgeois supérieurs*', and 327 '*Crus bourgeois*'. In 1966 there were 18 '*Crus exceptionnels*', 45 '*Grands bourgeois*' and 38 '*Crus bourgeois*'.

Some of the estates not mentioned in the 1932 classification were classed in 1966, others, either because of changes of ownership or divisions of property, were not included in the later classification. Again, it will be appreciated that use of the category of the classification on the label of the wine is a matter for the individual estate to decide, and also that many bourgeois growths have recently undergone radical rehabilitation, so that, even if you do not find the name of a particular wine in a list of classed growths of any kind, it may still be of excellent quality.

In general, it is probably fair to say that the classed growths of the Médoc, and the top classed growths of the Graves (red and white) and the St. Émilions (Pomerol has not yet been classified) are all wines of stature, marked individuality and tend to be more large-scale than others. As far as the classed growths of the Médoc are concerned, they tend to be slightly slower to mature than the majority of bourgeois growths. And, as might be expected, any estate that features in a classification tends to command a higher price for its wines.

The 1855 Classification of Red Wines (The names are given in the order in which they originally appeared.)

Premiers Crus

Ch. Lafite	Pauillac
Ch. Margaux	Margaux
Ch. Latour	Pauillac
Ch. Haut Brion	Pessac (Graves)
Ch. Mouton-Rothschild (since 1973)	Pauillac

Deuxièmes Crus

Ch. Rausan-Ségla	Margaux
Ch. Rauzan-Gassies	Margaux
Ch. Léoville-Lascases	St. Julien
Ch. Léoville-Poyferré	St. Julien
Ch. Léoville-Barton	St. Julien
Ch. Durfort-Vivens	Margaux
Ch. Lascombes	Margaux
Ch. Gruaud-Larose	St. Julien
Ch. Brane-Cantenac	Cantenac
Ch. Pichon-Longueville	Pauillac
Ch. Pichon-Longueville-Lalande	Pauillac
Ch. Ducru-Beaucaillou	St. Julien
Ch. Cos d'Estournel	St. Estèphe
Ch. Montrose	St. Estèphe

Troisièmes Crus

Ch. Kirwan	Cantenac
Ch. Issan	Cantenac
Ch. Lagrange	St. Julien
Ch. Langoa	St. Julien
Ch. Giscours	Labarde
Ch. Malescot-Saint-Exupéry	Margaux
Ch. Cantenac-Brown	Cantenac
Ch. Palmer	Cantenac
Ch. Grand la Lagune	Ludon
Ch. Calon-Ségur	St. Estèphe
Ch. Ferrière	Margaux
Ch. Marquis d'Alesme-Becker	Margaux
Ch. Boyd-Cantenac	Margaux

Quatrièmes Crus

Ch. Saint-Pierre-Sevaistre	St. Julien
Ch. Saint-Pierre-Bontemps	St. Julien

Ch. Branaire-Ducru	St. Julien
Ch. Talbot	St. Julien
Ch. Duhart-Milon	Pauillac
Ch. Poujet	Cantenac
Ch. La Tour Carnet	St. Laurent
Ch. Rochet	St. Estèphe
Ch. Beychevelle	St. Julien
Ch. Le Prieuré	Cantenac
Ch. Marquis de Terme	Margaux

Cinquièmes Crus

Ch. Pontet Canet	Pauillac
Ch. Batailley	Pauillac
Ch. Haut-Batailley	Pauillac
Ch. Grand-Puy-Lacoste	Pauillac
Ch. Grand-Puy-Ducasse	Pauillac
Ch. Lynch-Bages	Pauillac
Ch. Lynch-Moussas	Pauillac
Ch. Dauzac	Labarde
Ch. Mouton d'Armailhacq	Pauillac
(now Mouton Baron Philippe)	
Ch. Le Tertre	Arsac
Ch. Haut-Bages-Liberal	Pauillac
Ch. Pédesclaux	Pauillac
Ch. Belgrave	St. Laurent
Ch. Camensac	St. Laurent
Ch. Cos-Labory	St. Estèphe
Ch. Clerc-Milon	Pauillac
Ch. Croizet-Bages	Pauillac
Ch. Cantemerle	Macau

1855 Classification of White Wines

Grand Premier Crus

Ch. Yquem	Sauternes

Premiers Crus

Ch. La Tour Blanche	Bommes
Ch. Peyraguey (Clos Haut Peyraguey)	Bommes
(Lafaurie Peyraguey)	Bommes
Ch. Rayne-Vigneau	Bommes
Ch. de Suduiraut	Preignac
Ch. Coutet	Barsac
Ch. Climens	Barsac
Ch. Guiraud	Fargues
Ch. Rabaud (Rabaud-Promis)	Bommes
(Sigalas-Rabaud)	Bommes
Ch. de Myrat	Barsac
Ch. Doisy (Doisy-Dubroca)	Barsac
(Doisy-Daëne)	Barsac

(Doisy-Védrines)	Barsac
Ch. Peixotto	Bommes
Ch. d'Arche (and d'Arche-Lafauire)	Sauternes
Ch. Filhot	Sauternes
Ch. Broustet	Barsac
Ch. Nairac	Barsac
Ch. Caillou	Barsac
Ch. de Malle	Preignac
Ch. Raymond-Lafon	Fargues
Ch. Lamothe (Lamothe-Bergey)	Sauternes
(Lamothe-Espagnet)	Sauternes

1959 Classification of White Graves

Ch. Bouscaut	Cadaujac
Ch. La Tour Martillac	Martillac
Ch. Laville-Haut Brion	Talence
Ch. Couhins	Villenave-d'Ornon
Ch. Carbonnieux	Léognan
Ch. Olivier	Léognan
Domaine de Chevalier	Léognan
Ch. Malartic-Lagravière	Léognan

1953 Classification of Red Graves

Ch. Bouscaut	Cadaujac
Ch. Haut-Bailly	Léognan
Domaine de Chevalier	Léognan
Ch. Carbonnieux	Léognan
Ch. Fieuzal	Léognan
Ch. Malartic-Lagravière	Léognan
Ch. Olivier	Léognan
Ch. La Tour Martillac	Martillac
Ch. Smith-Haut-Lafitte	Martillac
Ch. Haut-Brion	Pessac
Ch. Pape Clément	Pessac
Ch. La Mission Haut-Brion	Talence
Ch. La Tour Haut-Brion	Talence

1955 Classification of Saint-Émilion

Premier Grand Cru Classé
Ch. Ausone
Ch. Beauséjour (Dufau)
Ch. Beauséjour (Fagouet)
Ch. Cheval Blanc
Ch. Belair
Ch. Canon
Ch. Figeac
Ch. la Gaffelière-Naudes
Ch. Magdelaine

Ch. Pavie
Ch. Trottevieille
Clos Fourtet

Grand Cru Classé
Ch. l'Arrosée
Ch. l'Angélus
Ch. Balestard-la-Tonnelle
Ch. Bellevue
Ch. Bergat
Ch. Cadet-Piola
Ch. Cadet-Bon
Ch. Canon-la-Gaffelière
Ch. Cap-de-Mourlin
Ch. Chapelle-Madeleine
Ch. Chauvin
Ch. Corbin
Ch. Coutet
Ch. Croque-Michotte
Ch. Curé-Bon
Ch. Fonplégade
Ch. Fonroque
Ch. Franc-Mayne
Ch. Grand Barrail
Ch. Grand-Corbin-Despagne
Ch. Grand-Corbin-Pécresse
Ch. Grand-Mayne
Ch. Grand-Pontet
Ch. Grandes-Murailles
Ch. Guadet-Saint-Julien
Ch. Jean-Faure
Ch. la Carte
Ch. la Clotte
Ch. la Clusière
Ch. la Couspaude
Ch. la Dominique
Ch. Larcis-Ducasse
Ch. Lamarzelle
Ch. Lamarzelle-Figeac
Ch. Larmande
Ch. Laroze
Ch. Lasserre
Ch. La Tour-du-Pin-Figeac
Ch. La Tour-Figeac
Ch. le Châtelet
Ch. le Couvent
Ch. le Prieuré
Ch. Mauvezin
Ch. Moulin du Cadet

Ch. Pavie-Décesse
Ch. Pavie-Macquin
Ch. Pavillon-Cadet
Ch. Petit-Faurie de Souchard
Ch. Faurie de Soutard
Ch. Ripeau
Ch. Sansonnet
Ch. Saint-Georges-Côte-Pavie
Ch. Soutard
Ch. Tertre-Daugay
Ch. Trimoulet
Ch. Trois-Moulins
Ch. Troplong-Mondot
Ch. Villemaurine
Ch. Yon Figeac
Clos des Jacobins
Clos la Madeleine
Clos Saint-Martin

5

Touring the Wine Regions

The Bordeaux region is so big and extensive that, in order to see all of it, at least five to eight days are necessary for a tour. It is unlikely, however, that even the most enthusiastic traveller will attempt, in the course of a single visit, to see details of every single vineyard division, as to do this in a short space of time would not only be extremely tiring but result in a confused mass of impressions, rather than clear ideas of the differences between the regions and memories of certain of the properties in them.

Motoring. Local transport is good: the long distance buses enable most places to be visited fairly quickly and cheaply, and the main towns are serviced by the provincial trains. Tour operators, of course, plan specific trips, and these can be excellent value, although of course the individual traveller is not free to make detours of his own in addition to the planned itinerary. But the ideal, as might be expected, is to have the use of a car, as the main roads are extremely good and can cut down the time of travel. It should be remembered, however, that Bordeaux itself is a very large and thickly populated city. So, if you have to begin your journey from the centre and go out, or if your route involves actually going through the city, the density of the traffic may put on half an hour or more to what might otherwise have been quite a short excursion. If you hesitate between hiring a self-drive or chauffeur-driven car, I would certainly advise the latter, unless you are very experienced in driving in Europe. The driver, incidentally, need not be a 'chauffeur'—he could be a student or a member of the hotel staff—and this form of transport can be cheaper than others for a visitor with limited time to spare.

You should also plan your itinerary beforehand: not only is the traffic heavy and complicated in parts of the city and at the big road junctions, but some of the side roads, from which the wine estates are best seen, are extremely confusing and you will waste time if you are continually having to stop and look at the map. In a car you can get close to certain of the great estates,

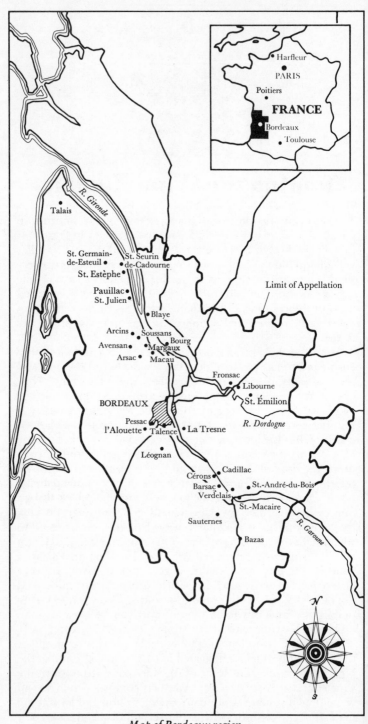

Map of Bordeaux region

and this is the best way of registering impressions. You can route yourself as an individual and stop when you like, to inspect vineyards and soil, as well as for the more obvious reasons of taking photographs or looking around in a picturesque town or village.

The big main roads and autoroutes, which are increasing everywhere, can get you quickly from one major centre to another, but, if you are in a stream of fast-moving traffic, you are unlikely to be able to devote much time to looking around you, and certainly on an autoroute you may hardly register that you are in wine country at all. So I suggest that, unless there is some reason for great haste, the routes followed should mostly be those that show the landscape and estates, even if they are neither fast nor in particularly good repair. It is difficult to give precise information on routes, mainly because of the amount of roadworks in progress in the region at the time of writing. You can, however, use the sketch maps in this book as general guidelines, and up-to-date Michelin maps numbers 71 and 75 will enable you to find your way about on even the smaller roads and tracks, avoiding any large-scale reconstructions of the road and the industrialised suburbs.

An up-to-date map, or maps, showing the autoroutes, is essential if you are not to risk being confused by a gigantic confluence of major roads, with lanes directing traffic into a number of places which you may never have heard of before. The number of the road, as well as the place you are making for, should be noted when you are preparing your trip. There are people who can look at a map over breakfast and keep the names of places and numbers of roads accurately in their mind for the rest of the day, but the ordinary traveller will find it wisest to jot down a list of places and road numbers.

If you do get lost, and have to ask the way, there is usually someone who can tell you the nearest *grande route* (main road) and its destination, but don't forget that you are in the country, and people from whom you make enquiries in a village may, in the whole of their lives, never have been to the next major town in the area, so that they will not always be able to give you helpful directions. A garage, of course, is the ideal place at which to ask the way, but if you don't speak even a little French, take the map and list of places you want to get to when you are trying to get help. And don't forget that the accent of the Gironde, which is oddly mewing, with words ending in '-in', '-ein', or '-en', all sounding as if they were written '-ang', with a considerable twang, may add to your difficulties. The accent of Marseilles is supposed to bewilder visitors, but as an ordinary tourist, I have never found it half so hard to make out as the *accent de la Flèche*. The 'Flèche' is the spire of the church of St. Michel, the tallest in the whole of the Midi or southern France, and is the Bordelais equivalent to 'the sound of Bow Bells'.

Tours in the Wine Regions

In following the various routes, refer to the descriptions (pages 49–58) as to what the wines are like in relation to the areas where they are produced. You will be able to make out the differences in the appearance of the countryside and the colour of the soils. In the itineraries things that are of particular historical as well as wine interest are indicated, so that those planning their individual routes can make the choice from the overall lists of places they want to see.

For those who have only a limited time at their disposal, the following are suggestions for tours that enable the visitor to see something of certain classic vineyards.

Only two-three hours maximum to spare. The estates of Haut Brion and La Mission Haut Brion are both at Pessac, and those of La Tour Haut Brion and Laville Haut Brion are at Talence. Leave Bordeaux on the N10 for Talence and Pessac, and, if there is time, turn right to join the N650 for l'Alouette, if you wish to see Pape Clément, the other great Graves estate.

About three hours, morning or afternoon. Take the road out of Bordeaux (D1), as for as Le Vigean, where you turn right on the D2, through Blanquefort, and up to Ludon and Macau. Continue on this road, from which you can see the vineyards of La Lagune and Cantemerle, and you will arrive at Labarde, Cantenac and Margaux. From the road itself, you can see Château Palmer, some of the vineyard of Château Margaux, the vineyards of Rausan-Ségla and Rauzan-Gassies, the entrance to Le Prieuré, the Lichine property, and Malescot-Saint-Exupéry; Château Lascombes is only just off the road. It would be possible to make this excursion in a morning or afternoon, cutting down the time to about two hours if you are staying at any of the hotels at Le Lac, north of Bordeaux, but allowing certainly more time if a start has to be made from the centre of Bordeaux or south of the city.

A whole morning and the lunch hour, or a long afternoon. Cross the river and go to Libourne, St. Émilion and Pomerol. If you start from Le Lac, take the new road through the Parc des Expositions and the Pont d'Angoulème to join the N89. Alternatively, starting from the centre of Bordeaux, take the Pont de Pierre and join the N89 after Cenon. This is a fast although very busy road. Allowing time for a meal, you will be able to see the pleasant town of Libourne and the extremely picturesque town of St. Émilion, with its two most important churches and many antiquities. If a detour is made after St. Émilion to Castillon, those who wish to go a little further can see St. Michel de Montaigne, or, returning by the N136, see something of the Entre-Deux-Mers and Premières Côtes, according to the time available.

About three hours. If you have previously seen other regions, you can use even this short time to go through the Graves, Sauternes and Barsac, leaving Bordeaux by the N113, possibly making a detour to see La Brède (see page 20) on the way, and then continuing to Podensac, with the choice then either to go on as far as Langon, or spend the time in the circuit of the Sauternais (see page 81). At Langon, you can cross the river into the Premières Côtes, returning through Ste. Croix du Mont, Cadillac and Longoiran and Quinsac to Bordeaux along the other bank of the Garonne. Those who wish to extend the journey beyond Langon have the possibilities of visiting the great Château of Villandraut, the superb church and parvis (enclosed area in front of the Cathedral) at Bazas and the impressive castle at Roquetaillade. The autoroute A61 runs from Le Pont de Maye down to just west of Langon, so this part of the journey can be shortened, if you wish.

A whole day. Devote the time to visiting the Médoc. Start by the route recommended to see Margaux (page 72), and continue through Soussans, Arcins, possibly making a detour to see the Fort Médoc (the ruins of a magnificent fortified estate on the banks of the river) then either Lamarque or Cussac. Then go on to St. Julien, Pauillac, up to St. Estèphe and beyond, through St. Seurin de Cadourne, to Château Loudenne (which is of particular interest as well as beauty, because it was bought by the Gilbey family just over a century ago and has remained in British hands ever since). The return can either be made by the same road, or one can turn off at a number of towns at any point from Lesparre down to the south, to join the fast main road, D1, which goes through St. Laurent de Médoc, Listrac, Moulis and Castelnau. This route will enable you to note the difference in the terrain.*

BOURG AND BLAYE.

This can make a pleasant half-day excursion, or slightly longer, depending at which point you cross the river. As far as the vineyards are concerned, they are on a smallish scale and not as impressive as in some of the other regions, but there is the magnificent Citadel of Blaye, designed by Vauban, the Château du Bouilh, a masterpiece of architecture by Victor Louis, built in the eighteenth century, although never finished, and the fiftieth latitude, which is near St. André de Cubzac, affording a good panorama over the Dordogne valley. Lormont, across the river from Bordeaux, where Richard of Bordeaux is supposed to have been born in the castle, is a pleasant riverside little town.

The Estates

It is obviously impossible, in a book of this size, to give the

---

*For details of the properties seen on this or the other trips, note the specific regional itineraries.

history of even the classed growths. What I have chosen to do here, therefore, is to provide notes on those estates which are both particularly famous and well known for various reasons to the English-speaking drinker, and to include with these any additional information on properties that are conspicuous or easily viewed from a road or lane that the traveller may take. Much additional historical and general background material will of course be available for visitors shown round an estate, but the following may give an idea to those planning a tour as to which properties are likely to be most interesting to them.

THE MÉDOC

It is possible that the word Médoc is a contraction of the Latin *in medio aquae*—in the midst of the waters. The local proverb, "in the Médoc the vine likes to see the river", has already been mentioned, and the Gironde is certainly seldom out of sight of the greater estates.

From the point of view of the wine lover, this is possibly the most important Bordeaux excursion, although the countryside is not impressive. If possible, try to allow time for a detour to see the *palus*, or river bank vineyards, east of the main wine road up the Médoc, and, in arranging a detailed visit to two or more estates, try to choose properties in different parishes, so that it is possible to note the regional differences in the wines.

MARGAUX AND CANTENAC

Just past the church in Cantenac is Château Prieuré Lichine, on the main road, which Alexis Lichine bought for his personal use. It has a particularly attractive farmhouse-style kitchen.

Château Margaux lies a little to the right of the D2, before the entrance to the town of Margaux, and just beyond the little pepperpot-towered church. It is an outstandingly beautiful building, in First Empire classical style, built by Combes, a pupil of Victor Louis; the *chais*, especially the first year *chai*, a majestically pillared hall, are equally impressive. But you can get a good view of the front of the Château from the wrought iron gate leading down the avenue to the colonnaded staircase and façade. In the Margaux vineyard note the light stony soil. Some of these stones can be polished up so as to glitter and shine and one of the past owners of Château Margaux, Count d'Hargicourt, godson of Madame Dubarry, once appeared at the Court of Louis XV wearing enormous lustrous buttons which attracted the attention of the King, who was told, when he asked about them, that d'Hargicourt was wearing 'the diamonds of my estate'. (But this story is also told about Château Latour.)

The Palmer vineyard is across the vineyard track from Château Mârgaux, and the three flags that are often flown on its turreted roof signify the joint ownership by a French, Dutch and English firm (the French family Miailhe, the Dutch Mähler-Besse, and Sichel, of London, Mainz and Bordeaux). For some of the history of Palmer see page 23, but wine writer Julian Jeffs tells the pleasant tale of how Sir Charles Palmer tried to make the wine of his estate fashionable by serving it at Carlton House, at a dinner presided over by the Prince Regent; unfortunately, one of the company denounced the elegant, delicate wine, saying that he preferred a claret from a smart wine merchant of the time (which had been considerably touched up with strong southern wines) and, as the company were comparing the two while eating anchovy sandwiches—a more unsuitable accompaniment for fine wine can hardly be imagined—the Palmer did not show well. Its owner, furious, nearly fought a duel with the thoughtless critic.

Across the road from Palmer are Rausan-Ségla and Rauzan-Gassies, side by side. Originally the properties were united, and their history can be traced at least to the seventeenth century, when they belonged to a wealthy wine merchant. They were divided at the time of the French Revolution, at the end of the eighteenth century. Rausan-Ségla today belongs to John Holt of Liverpool, owners also of the great Bordeaux wine-shipping firm of Eschenauer. Malescot St. Exupéry, in the main street of Margaux, gets its unusual name from Simon Malescot, Procureur of the Court at the Parliament of Bordeaux, who bought it in 1697. In 1827 it was acquired by Count Jean-Baptiste de St. Exupéry, the great-grandfather of the famous writer, Antoine de Saint-Exupéry, author of many books about flying. Only a little removed from the very centre of Margaux is Château Lascombes, now owned by the British brewery and wine firm, Bass Charrington Vintners, and formerly by Alexis Lichine, who used it for holding annual art exhibitions of modern paintings to do with wine and vines. Both Palmer and Lascombes, on account of their associations with Great Britain, and the admirable organisation of their *chais*, are particularly worth visiting.

There are a number of other estates worth looking at, if you can make a detour, even if it is only possible to see the building from a gateway or the vineyard from the side of the road. These include La Lagune at Ludon, Cantemerle at Macau, Giscours at Labarde, d'Issan at Margaux* and the two bourgeois growths, La Tour de Mons at Labarde, owned by the proprietor of Cantemerle, and d'Angludet at Cantenac, the last being the home of Peter Sichel† and his family.

*One of the Cruse family homes; another, La Dame Blanche, is a very beautiful property at Le Taillan.

†Head of Maison Sichel Bordeaux, who are one of the owners of Palmer, and the first person not of French nationality to become Président of the Bordeaux Syndicate.

ST. JULIEN

Château Beychevelle is at the very entrance to the St. Julien vineyard, a very handsome estate with beautiful gardens. Originally the Château du Médoc, it became known as Beychevelle when the Grand Admiral of France, the Duc d'Epernon, acquired the estate in 1587 and commanded all the ships passing the property on the river to strike their sails as a mark of respect—"baisser les voiles".

Along the road past Beychevelle are the vineyards of Châteaux Langoa and Léoville-Barton, the latter once forming part of a huge vineyard with Léoville-Poyferré and Léoville-Lascases south and north of St. Julien-Beychevelle further on. There is no château at Léoville-Barton, the wine being made in the *chais* at Langoa, but Château Langoa, although the wine is never quite on a level with that of Léoville-Barton, is an enchanting building, built in 1759, with the cellar directly under the terrace and front door, and it can be seen from the road. It has belonged to the Anglo-Irish family of Barton since 1821. The Bartons have been in the Bordeaux wine trade since the beginning of the eighteenth century.

As Cyril Ray points out, in his history of the Langoa-Léoville-Barton vineyards, "no classified wine-growing château has been for so long in the hands of the same family as has Château Langoa-Barton", and referring to the 1855 classification, he notes that, of the owners, "only two are the same now as then . . . Rothschild and Barton." Throughout their Bordeaux history, the Bartons never married into France, in other words, they have taken their brides from other nationalities than the country in which they have lived.

The Léoville-Lascases vineyard is notable for its great gate, which features on the label, the present owners being descendants of the Marquis de Léoville, who acquired the estate in 1712. Note that the vineyard is on the very edge of the boundary between St. Julien and Pauillac, which means that the wines often have some of the Pauillac characteristics (see pages 56–57).

Other estates, not so easily seen, but worth visiting, are Château Ducru-Beaucaillou, which is not only impressive to look at, but has one of the few real cellars, where the bottled wines are kept just below ground, in the Médoc. Château Gruaud Larose, the turreted La Tour Carnet, and Talbot are others.

PAUILLAC

Château Latour today belongs mainly to the Pearson Group of London, Harveys of Bristol, and some French owners. In the eighteenth century, the Marquis de Ségur, known fairly enough as 'le Prince des Vignes', owned Latour, Lafite, Mouton, Calon-Ségur and other properties. He, and the owners of

Château Margaux, were the most important Gironde victims of the French Revolution and went to the guillotine in Paris. But Latour has a longer history than that: the original of the present dumpy tower, from which the estate takes its name, was

Tower at Château Latour

once part of a line of look-outs along the river in Plantagenet times.* Since its reacquisition by the English in 1962, the vineyard and *chais* have been enormously improved, the particular type of stainless steel vats at Latour having been among the first in the Gironde.

On opposite sides of the road are the two Pichon estates, which were once united, under the Baron de Longueville, who was the first Président of the Bordeaux parliament in the seventeenth century. Louis XIV was supposed to have stayed at Pichon (although not in the present buildings) when he was going down to the Pyrenees to be married to the Infanta of Spain. The estate was divided in 1850, and the Comtesse de Lalande, one of the Baron de Pichon's sisters, shared the estate that is now associated with her name with her other two sisters. The two Pichons are quite different, and although I happen to think that Pichon Lalande tends to be a more charming, light and elegant wine today, the Baron is also a very fine one. As an aide-mémoire, if you have a rather vulgar mind, it may be pertinent to remember that Pichon Baron is the château with the tall, conically pointed towers, whereas Pichon Lalande, 'the lady', is flat topped.

Further up the road, the vineyard of Lynch-Bages is a reminder of one of the number of Irish families (Lynch) who have settled in the Bordeaux region. On the quayside of

*The present tower is certainly of a later date.

Pauillac itself is Grand Puy Ducasse, which now contains a small wine museum and is the headquarters of the wine order of the region*. The traveller should avoid the horrors of the Shell refinery on the outskirts of Pauillac, which was established before the war, but which has now been so extended that recently enormous publicity was given to '*Château d'Huile*', because it was feared that the stench and aerial deposits would harm the adjacent vineyards. It is certainly an atrocity and, as the owners of the great estates must certainly have been influential enough to limit the expansion of something that could perfectly well have been situated other than in the heart of the greatest wine growing region of France, as well as being an eyesore in the countryside anyway, it must be considered merely a matter of luck that so far the beastly installations do not appear to have harmed either the vineyards or the wine of the great estates, though they are repellent to the view.

Continue on the D2, from which a number of great estates are signposted, but after Le Pouyalet the road winds round to give a superb view straight across the vineyard and on to the front of the Château of Lafite. The history of this wonderful estate has been written elegantly by Cyril Ray, and even the Revolutionary Government in France, offering it for sale in 1796–97, described it as "La domaine de Lafite, premier cru de Médoc et produisant le premier vin de Bordeaux". In 1821 it was owned by Sir Samuel Scott, a banker, in a firm which later became the Westminster Bank; but there was some doubt as to who really owned it, and a family called Vanlerberghe, a member of whom had actually bought it in 1803, put it up for sale again in 1856, when it was purchased by Baron James de Rothschild. The label on bottles of Lafite today shows the château as it was at the time of the purchase, and the château has hardly changed in the course of a century. At first you may not notice the five arrows, which form the weather vane on the top of the pepperpot tower. These are symbolic of the five brothers of the house of Rothschild—the brothers who established the family fortunes from their beginnings in the ghetto in Frankfurt in the late eighteenth century.

In Le Pouyalet, the traveller will see the turnings to Mouton Rothschild, Mouton Baron Philippe and Pontet-Canet, and the wonderful museum of works of art concerned with wine at Mouton, as well as the extremely impressive *chais*, certainly merits a detour. Pontet-Canet, one of the largest estates, is also unusual in that the grapes are received on an upper floor of the *chai* from which there is a most impressive view of the vineyards. Grand Puy-Lacoste, on a slightly elevated area behind Pauillac, and Batailley, the name of which is supposed

---

*The Commanderie du Bontemps du Médoc et des Graves. The '*bontemps*', which is the toque-like hat of members, has a white top, for a *bontemps* is the wooden bowl in which egg whites used to be mixed for finings.

Chai at Château Lafite

to commemorate a battle fought by the soldiers of Bertrand du Guesclin against the English, are other properties making fine wines, and should be visited if possible, although they have an unpretentious look as far as the châteaux themselves are concerned.

ST. ESTÈPHE

Still on the D2, continue past Château Lafite Rothschild and turn left up the steepish slope towards St. Estèphe. At the top of this little hill is Cos d'Estournel,• a riot of Médocain chinoiserie, built by Louis Gaspard d'Estournel, at the beginning of the nineteenth century, out of fondness for the east (he also bought and sold Arab horses as well as wine). The advantageous situation is such that, during the last war, the Germans mounted a gun emplacement on the top of the château to command the estuary (they also stole the gold temple bells from the pagodas), and it is one more astonishing thing about this odd looking building that the ornate door, which came from the palace of the Sultans of Zanzibar, leads not into a château at all, but simply into the *chais*. Cos d'Estournel makes an invariably fine wine, and, when Cyril Ray was writing his book on Lafite he found to his astonishment that both the staff and some of the executives at Lafite said that they would prefer to drink Cos d'Estournel if they could not drink Lafite! There is a great contrast in the two styles, but Cos d'Estournel, although somewhat austere and reserved, has a tradition for very fine wines. Alongside, divided only by the road, is Cos Labory, which once formed part

---

•'Cos', which may refer to the enclosure—*clos* or *caux*, an ancient form of the word *côte* or slope—is pronounced like the 'cos' in 'cos lettuce', with the final 's' sounded. This is one more instance of Bordelais pronunciation not being wholly French, and I have often wondered whether this particular sounding of the final letter does not relate to the time of the English occupation.

of the same estate, owned by a James Martyn of London in the nineteenth century.

On the plateau, after the turning to Marbuzet, where several good bourgeois growths are made, there is a good view of the recently rehabilitated Lafon-Rochet, now the property of Guy Tesseron, whose wife is a member of the Cruse family, one of the largest and most important of the Bordeaux wine dynasties. A detour off the D2 can lead to Montrose (the 't' is not sounded if you are speaking French, but can be when you speak English). The 'rose' part of its name describes the heather that used to cover the slope on which the property stands; Montrose has nothing to do with the town of that name in Scotland.

Calon-Ségur gets its name from the 'calones', the little boats that were used on the river and the latter part from the Marquis de Ségur, who is supposed to have said, referring to some of his properties, "I make wine at Lafite and Latour, but my heart lies at Calon". This is why Calon-Ségur has a heart on its label today. There are several excellent bourgeois growths making wine in St. Estèphe, notably Château de Pez, and Les Ormes de Pez. The visitor will find them very near to the centre of the village of Pez itself.

CHATEAU LOUDENNE

If time permits, continue from the St. Estèphe vineyard northward so as to pass through St. Seurin de Cadourne, and from there continue to the turn of the D2, taking the route to Château Loudenne. This property was bought in 1875 by the Gilbey brothers, who wanted to provide themselves with a Bordeaux base for shipping, as well as for growing wine; this is why they constructed the magnificent *chais*, and even a small harbour, though this last is no longer used. The pink château itself, with a wonderful view over part of the vineyards and the river, is used today as a reception and guest house for privileged friends of Gilbey Vintners, and, like Lascombes and Latour, is a substantial living refutation of the 'big is bad' theory about the British wine trade, for these three estates have had enormous sums put into them by the owning companies, to the benefit not only of guests and staff, but also to the vineyard and the estate wines. Loudenne is a substantial concern today, as it handles the enormous stocks of Gilbey France, which extend far beyond Bordeaux, if these are being put through the property en route to an export market. The purchases of château wines stored in the chais are gigantic. Loudenne is well organised to receive visitors, though if possible an appointment should be made if you wish to be shown round.

It is then possible to follow a cross-country route, possibly through Vertheuil, after returning to St. Seurin de Cadourne, or you can make straight for the town of Lesparre and the big main road, and then return to Bordeaux through St. Laurent de Médoc by a faster road, which passes through Listrac, Moulis, and Castelnau, from which detours may be made to see the properties of the region.

ST. ÉMILION, POMEROL, FRONSAC

The choice of route for this trip depends on whether you are going to cross the river from Bordeaux itself, or by the new bridge, and if there is time to visit Pomerol as well as St. Émilion. The N89 goes from Bordeaux to Libourne, the town named after Roger de Leybourne,* in the middle ages. With its arcades, it is an attractive place to stop, and the restaurant Loubat is still owned by the family into which a young woman married a considerable time ago; when her husband bought part of the Pétrus estate in 1925, she interested herself particularly in this, buying the whole of it in the mid-1940s. Madame Loubat's devotion to Château Pétrus resulted in the estate achieving pre-eminence above all other Pomerols, good though they may be.

Even after her death (the estate is now owned by the firm of Moueix), the price the wine of Pétrus fetches is up to and sometimes level with the first growths of the Médoc. The vineyard was virtually destroyed by the frosts of 1956, and there is a picture of Madame Loubat showing a glass from the sole cask of wine that was the result of the subsequent vintage. She refused to replant, and today her confidence in the estate is well justified.

The Pomerol vineyard is not large, and it is therefore worth while making detours to see, if possible, Vieux-Château-Certan, Certan, La Conseillante, Petit-Villages, l'Evangile, Gazin, La Pointe and Clos René. Beyond Pomerol there are the vineyards of Lalande de Pomerol and Néac, for the traveller who can go a little further.

The Fronsac vineyard is situated on a definite hill, something unusual in the Bordeaux vineyard, and overlooks the valleys of the rivers Isle and Dordogne, which join at the foot of it. To see Fronsac, turn off the N89 at the bridge leading into Libourne, bearing left, and follow the N670.

The St. Émilion vineyard is more extensive, but if you are in the area for the first time, you should certainly visit St. Émilion the town, and allow at least an hour to walk about, to appreciate the beauty and quaintness of the most picturesque wine town in this part of France. Also worth visiting are the Collegial Church, in which the Vintage Mass is held every autumn, the Maison du Vin, the ruined Cordeliers cloisters, the astonishing 'monolithic' church, unique in every way, in the

*Seneschal of Gascony, who built the castle and gave the town—founded in 1270 by Edward I of England—his own name.

lower part of the town, and the cave in which the unfortunate Girondins, victims of the Terror that they themselves had helped to unleash, were discovered after they had hoped to escape. The macaroons, which are a local speciality, are also worth sampling.

The great growth of St. Émilion is Cheval Blanc, almost in Pomerol, just off the D21, and near Pétrus. But if you wish to remain in or near St. Émilion and there is time to spare, it is possible to make short excursions on foot to a number of properties actually on the slope of the hillside, with cellars dug deep into the rocky outcrop. The most impressive of these is perhaps Clos Fourtet, where there are several storeys of galleries dug out of the rock, but Château Ausone, a little lower down, and commemorating the poet Ausonius, is another. Many of the St. Émilion estates are very picturesque, and wine-lovers will enjoy wandering about through the vineyard tracks and making the acquaintance of many great and popular wines on the spot. Also to be noted are the stone lines between which vines were planted in Roman times.

If there is time to spare, go further east, to Castillon-la-Bataille, where there is the monument to the Earl of Talbot who fell when the English were defeated by the French in 1453, and a little further along the N136, detour to see St. Michel de Montaigne (see page 18). It is possible to return to Bordeaux by taking the N136 from St. Pey d'Armens, instead of going back via Libourne, and from Branne a further detour may be made into the Entre Deux Mers down as far as the Premières Côtes in the valley of the Garonne. The countryside is particularly attractive, but the roads are small and winding, so that it is impossible to hurry, although anyone with a long day to spare might well go down as far as Langon from the north and return through the Premières Côtes and Entre Deux Mers to Bordeaux.

GRAVES, CÉRONS, SAUTERNES, BARSAC, LOUPIAC, SAINTE-CROIX-DU-MONT, THE ENTRE DEUX MERS, SAINTE-CROIX BORDEAUX, AND GRAVES DE VAYRES

If you are limited for time, take the autoroute to Langon, from the south of Bordeaux, and work back through the Graves, Sauternais and Barsac. Otherwise, take the N113 from the south of Bordeaux, including the great estates of Haut Brion, Pape Clément, and La Mission Haut Brion if possible. Haut Brion belonged to the Pontac family from the sixteenth century until 1935. A son of the Mayor of Bordeaux, François Auguste de Pontac, opened a tavern in London called Pontac's Head in 1666, and the wine became well-known to London, although Pepys had drunk "Ho Bryen" as early as 1663. In 1935, the American Clarence Dillon bought the estate and it now belongs to his son.

Haut Brion is very impressive to visit and the stainless steel fermentation tanks were installed as early as 1961. Many traditional makers of claret wrung their hands and said this was the end, but now nearly all of them make use of stainless steel. Across the road from Haut Brion is La Mission Haut Brion, originally part of the Haut Brion estate, but left to a religious order in 1682. It now belongs to the Woltner family. The wines are of particular elegance and beauty.

Nearest of all to Bordeaux, at l'Alouette, is Pape Clément, which commemorates the former Archbishop of Bordeaux, Bertrand de Got, who was elected Pope as Clement V in 1305. It was this pope who was obliged to move from Rome to Avignon in the complicated quarrels over the papacy, but Pope Clement V definitely had his vineyards where Pape Clément now stands. Other estates well worth visiting, and not far from Bordeaux include Château Carbonnieux, Domaine de Chevalier, and the well-known estates Olivier and Malartic-Lagravière. The estates of Smith-Haut-Lafitte and Bouscaut have recently undergone considerable rehabilitation.

Barsac is the first great sweet wine area entered when travelling south, and here it is also possible to cross the Garonne, leaving the region of Cérons and making for Cadillac. Further on, it is possible to make the excursion of the Sauternais circuit, starting near Langon, where you come off the autoroute and rejoin the N113. The Sauternais and Barsac regions are comparatively small and compact, and the route is signposted at several places. However, the countryside is undulating and inclined to be closed in, and if you are short of time, the risk of getting lost is great. I have been round this region a number of times driving myself, also driving with members of the wine trade and brokers, and in no instance has anyone actually got from one point to the other by the route originally expected! You may see a signpost which indicates two places of the same name pointing in totally opposite directions! However, distances are not great, and even to attempt this circuit is worthwhile.

In addition to the great Château d'Yquem, which is useful as a landmark, because it stands high on a hill, it is easy to see the very beautiful Château de Malle, and actually pass through the grounds of the charming Château Filhot, as the road crosses the front of the château. The great estates to look out for, in addition to those mentioned, include Coutet, Climens, Lafaurie-Peyraguey, Rieussec, Suduiraut and Rayne-Vigneau. Mention has been made (pages 80–81) of other excusions that may be made from any visit to this region.

From Langon, you can go further along the N113, which crosses the river, through St. Macaire, as far as La Réole and, if you wish, to Marmande. A more circuitous route from Langon leads through Auros on the D10 and subsequent side roads, via the D12 back to La Réole, or by way of the D10 from outside Auros down into Aillas, Aillas-Vieux and St. Sauveur de Meilhan, from where it is possible to go on to Marmande or back to La Réole. This is not the Bordeaux vineyard but the Marmandais, where good red and white wines are increasingly being made, although as yet little known on export lists. The countryside is enchanting.

From Langon, the river may be crossed to the Sainte-Croix-du-Mont region, with a possible detour to Verdelais (see page 52) and then return through Cadillac. There the great Château of the Ducs d'Épernon should be seen, and note taken of the white wines of Loupiac, Monprinblanc, and, beyond Cadillac, Rions. The D10 that goes on the river bank from St. Macaire back to Cenon, opposite Bordeaux, is attractive, though narrow and winding. Unfortunately no detours can be made without taking up a considerable amount of extra time, but it is worth noting the white soil and chalky outcrops that rise above the road and in which many of the winemakers keep their stocks. This is also a particularly attractive region for restaurants situated along the river at Quinsac and La Tresne.

BLAYAIS, BOURGEAIS, CUBZAGUAIS

This is an attractive excursion which can be made either from central Bordeaux or by turning off the autoroute, having first crossed the river by the Pont d'Angoulème. The Bourg region is sometimes flatteringly called 'the Switzerland of the Gironde', because the countryside is particularly hilly. From Blaye, notably from the great citadel of Blaye (see page 49) a wonderful view of the Gironde may be enjoyed, including the churches of the parishes of St. Julien and Pauillac. Around St. André de Cubzac, just off what was formerly the major road from Bordeaux to Paris, pleasant red and white wines are made, and the region provides agreeable unhurried motoring for anyone who already knows the other main regions of the Gironde.

BORDEAUX

It is a pity if visitors neglect the city of Bordeaux itself, because there are many things to see within it that relate to the history of wine. Drive along the quays, from the Rostral Columns at the end of the Place des Quinconces, noting the old and beautiful houses, especially those in the elegant Cours Xavier Arnozan, and of the Quai des Chartrons and Quai du Baccalan. Turn back into the city, noting the elegant walks and avenues alongside the Jardin Publique and the Allées de Tourny and Place Tourny, and the Place Gambetta at the junction of the Cours de l'Intendance and Cours Georges Clemenceau. South of the Quinconces, the magnificent Place de la Bourse and subsequent quayside will lead to the quarter of the Salinières, the area where medieval tradesmen salted fish and meat. Behind this can be seen the narrow streets of one of the oldest parts of Bordeaux, and the great Porte de Cailhau, last-remaining fragment of the Palace of the Kings of England, on the quayside.

A little further on, the huge Cours de l'Alsace Lorraine leads past the dumpy Grosse Cloche, with its bell, where the Jurade de Bordeaux (the governing body) formerly had its seat, the Jurade's church being alongside and still standing. Between the Grosse Cloche and the river there are innumerable winding streets that are completely 'old Bordeaux' and in the Salinières district the town house of Michel de Montaigne (see page 18) may still be seen. Around the Cathedral of St. André itself, the beautiful houses, now mostly municipal buildings, indicate the prosperity of seventeenth- and eighteenth-century Bordeaux. The exquisite theatre in the Place de la Comédie should also be seen if possible, as it is one of the few built to enable people to parade about, display themselves and converse, in the intervals of the spectacle. This is a Bordeaux excursion which can only be made partly by mechanical means: ideally, stop and walk about at the Porte de Cailhau, the Grosse Cloche, and see the Cathedral, returning on foot. Take side roads and some of the pedestrian precincts to the Place de la Comédie, so as to gain an idea of what old Bordeaux was like.

Visiting Wine Estates

Although many properties put up notices saying "Visitez" or "Visitez les chais" this cannot be taken as an infallible invitation to be shown round. Obviously, it isn't practicable for chance travellers to be received at any time and in fact many of the big properties, including the first growths, do not permit the entrance of visitors to their *chais* or even to their reception rooms at vintage time, when the picking of the grapes and making of the wine has prior claim.

At other times of the year, an estate that has some kind of board up indicating that it may be open will usually have somebody around who can open the *chais*, although it must never be assumed that whoever does this—even the owner—will speak English. The usual procedure is for the visitor to be shown the first and second year *chais* and cast an eye around the nearest bit of the vineyard; sometimes a château will have a reception room in which pictures of the estate, vineyard implements and historic bottles and documents will be displayed.

You will not, as a casual visitor, invariably be given the opportunity to taste either the first or second year wine from the casks in which it is maturing, and it is rare indeed that you will be offered anything that is actually for drinking. A bottle of wine is unlikely to be opened in the *chais*, for visitors will usually be taken to some form of reception room. The vast numbers of visitors who pass through even the more modest châteaux during a year can make a substantial inroad on the stocks, which is why only those specially privileged (personal guests of the owner or important visitors guided at least by the owner of another property or head of a firm) are nowadays allowed to sample any of the first growths from the cask—the wine is simply too expensive to permit of its being offered around.* Even the drags of a glass will be carefully poured back into the cask or, in the second year *chai*, put by for restoring to the *grand vin* (the principal wine). This procedure is also followed by many other growths today.

But if you are able to speak a little French, and your interest is sincere, you can certainly venture to take at face value the notice inviting you to visit. When you have been shown round, you may be asked to sign the visitors' book, if the estate has such a thing in the reception area, and sometimes may be given a postcard or label of the estate. It is, naturally, thoughtless and ill-mannered to be greedy about this kind of souvenir, although people do go off with the most astonishing things. One supposedly sincere (and certainly privileged) wine lover who was taken round the Lafite *chais*, actually removed one of the silver taps from a cask! If you are not offered the chance to taste, don't ask—and, even if you are, don't make this the occasion for asking that your entire family should also have a sample. They are unlikely to enjoy drinking the young wine and are thereby only depriving the serious student—and potential customer—of the chance of trying it. Let them share your sample, if they must.

Ideally, get some kind of introduction before visiting any estates. But bear in mind that, although all *chais*, cellars and vineyards are fascinating to the wine lover, they may not be of more than passing interest to any accompanying family and friends. Although all estates are different from each other, it is fair to say that superficially there isn't much to occupy the ordinary traveller by touring several properties. So, unless you can park the less wine-minded somewhere, it is considerate only to plan on seeing in detail no more than perhaps two estates in the course of a morning or afternoon—and don't forget that the sacred French lunch hour means that no visitors will be received for a couple of hours either from midday or from one o'clock.

In fact, there is plenty to learn by looking around in the vineyards, noting differences in soil, aspect and the way the vines are cultivated and laid out, as well as seeing a number of great châteaux quite well from the outside (ordinary visitors do not get shown the interiors as a rule), so that even an extensive

---

* At Château Margaux, for example, it has been estimated that visitors' tasting samples swallowed up 16 caskfuls annually!

tour can still be interesting and varied. Local cafés and bars will usually be able to give you the locality's regional wine by the glass, for registering impressions of it on the spot.

Introductions to see specific estates can be arranged in various ways: the C.I.V.B. (Comité International du Vin de Bordeaux, 3, Cours du XXX Juillet) will, if given reasonable warning, arrange for authenticated groups of wine lovers, such as clubs, messes, members of trade associations and trade students to see round various properties. But they cannot do much for the ordinary tourist. However, the C.I.V.B. and the Syndicat d'Initiative (corner of the Allées de Tourney, Cours du XXX Juillet) and opposite the C.I.V.B., right in the centre of Bordeaux, can give information about which estates are open to visitors on Saturdays. Tour operators, of course, may include visits to certain properties in their itineraries and naturally the larger hotels may also be able to tell the visitor how to see certain estates (not all are open all the year round, even if they do display noticeboards of the "Visitez!" type).

The most agreeable and, often, the most practical way to see an estate, is by getting the introduction arranged through a wine merchant in the U.K. He can often contact a shipper with whom he deals, and arrange for the interested customer (it should really be someone who does buy wine, not simply the person who wants some free entertainment) to visit the shipper's establishment in the Gironde. There the visitor may be able to taste wines in the tasting room. Many of the shippers nowadays have staff who specialise in helping and, sometimes, escorting visitors around in the region. Even if there isn't anyone available for this purpose, a shipper can, on request, usually fix a visit to any particular property, so that you can be directed where to go, and have then only to keep the appointment. Remember that cellars are usually shut for the whole of August, although there may be office staff on duty.

It goes without saying—or should do—that if an arrangement is made in the U.K. that you will be at the shipper's office on such-and-such a morning or afternoon, you should be there, and be punctual. Failure to turn up may mean that somebody detailed to look after you is kept hanging about and wasting time, possibly at a busy season. If an appointment has to be cancelled, this should be done by telephone. If your French is not good enough to make the call, a garage, bar, café or hotel can be asked to help. Unfortunately, every shipper can tell stories of the thoughtlessness and bad manners of people who don't turn up, or who time their arrival to within minutes of the lunch break—hoping for a free meal—or who cause much inconvenience by wanting to taste a number of wines when at an estate, or taking up a lot of time of the staff there who may be fully occupied with their work. Everyone is delighted to welcome the interested and considerate lover of wine, though kindness and hospitality should never be taken for granted. But the visitor is an ambassador for his or her country and should bear this in mind.

Naturally, you thank whoever spends time on helping or showing you round. Remember that the French shake hands when greeting and bidding farewell, although a workman, or someone whose hands are dirty, will proffer a forearm out of care for the visitor's clean hands. And don't be misled by the person wearing a beret, ancient espadrilles and *bleus de travail* (jeans or overalls)—he may only be a workman, but he can be the *maître de chai* (cellarmaster), the *régisseur* (bailiff) or even the multi-millionaire owner of the property. He may speak better English than you do, having had an English nanny and been educated at an English school and university—so don't assume he doesn't understand what visitors say!

Traditionally, the visitor who arrives at an estate with an introduction is a privileged guest (whether or not the visit concludes with a glass of wine, as it sometimes does) and therefore a sincere expression of thanks before leaving is all that is required. Recently I read a guidebook that advised visitors to tip whoever shows them round at an estate; if the guide is merely a guide, and makes it clear that a tip is expected, then obviously some money must pass. However, I was always firmly instructed, when I was showing people round, that it is the height of bad manners to tip anybody else: anyone of the status of the *maître de chai* of a classed growth and above can probably buy up the average visitor several times over! Obviously circumstances can vary—but, if in doubt, don't.

Buying Wine in Bordeaux

At the bigger properties, you will certainly not be able to buy the wine direct, because it will be bespoken by shippers and merchants and brokers. The broker usually negotiates the deal between grower and shipper, getting 2 per cent for his trouble. However, at some small properties which do not sell to export markets or which can arrange sales of single cases, it may be possible to buy a dozen bottles for yourself. Do not forget that you will have to pay the duty when you bring the wine into the U.K., and that you should secure a detailed bill when you buy it.

In recent times sales of wine 'direct' are sometimes a feature of a visit to a property, but it's worth asking why? If the wine is all that good or a true bargain, isn't it unlikely that an estate of any standing will be unable to market it conventionally, instead of flogging it as a type of souvenir? Beware about this.

If you want to buy a particular wine while it is still young—and before the price may have risen—the wise procedure is to ask whoever is your contact at the shipper's establishment to tell you how to do this through the nearest agent in your homeland. If they sell to several outlets, they can inform you, and let you know the one most convenient to you. The staff at the estate may not know who exactly has bought the wine unless it is the monopoly of a particular establishment or establishments, as when a property is joint-owned. But the way to buy is, ideally, via a merchant through whom the transaction may be effected for you.

Wines of the locality are also often on sale at the various *Maisons du Vin* throughout the Gironde; these establishments, sometimes associated with a group of growers or the local mairie and council, may offer wines in quantities of less than a dozen bottles. There are also, of course, opportunities for buying wine in certain shops, or such local cafés and restaurants as can provide this service. However, choice may be very restricted and, if you study the prices of an establishment such as the Vinothèque, which is next to the Syndicat d'Initiative in Bordeaux itself, you'll realise that you might do better to save your francs and do your wine buying at home.

Other Drinks

Wine is not the only alcoholic beverage made in and around Bordeaux, although naturally it is the star. But there are several establishments that are worth knowing about, and some of them are well organised to receive visitors.

Marie Brizard. The liqueur establishment of Marie Brizard et Roger is an imposing, modern installation, but it is over 200 years old and its founder was one of the outstanding women of Bordeaux. Marie Brizard was born in the city in 1714 and, like other women of compassion and energy, did a considerable amount of work among the poor and sick. One of those whom she was able to help was a planter recently returned to his native land from West Africa, who, in gratitude, gave her his most precious possession—a drink that he had found efficacious in both preventing stomach upsets and curing them. Most experienced travellers today still have their favourite mixtures for this kind of trouble, and to share an efficacious prescription is a mark of true friendship.

Marie Brizard had the drink made up and found it extremely useful in her charitable work. The chief ingredient was aniseed, a herb used in treating stomach upsets since ancient times—the sixteenth-century English herbalist, John Gerard (1545–1612) recommended it as "good against belchings and upbraidings of the stomacke". Marie Brizard realised that this recipe was capable of commercial exploitation and had the idea of giving some to the then Governor of Bordeaux, the notorious Duc de Richelieu, who, in the course of his hectic life, combining politics, war, and a stream of seductions in addition to several marriages, must have appreciated anything that aided digestion—anyway, he lived to the age of 92 years 5 months, dying in 1788. Richelieu made the aniseed-based drink popular at the French Court, and Louis XV, who was quite gastronomically inclined, also enjoyed it, so that Marie Brizard was able to found the firm of Marie Brizard et Roger in 1755. Her partner, Jean-Baptiste Roger, was the husband of one of her nieces. Most liqueur houses make some kind of aniseed drink nowadays, but the anisette of Marie Brizard is still supposed to be the finest: as well as being a digestive, for drinking at the end of a meal, in which form the Briton will probably best know it, it can be served as an apéritif or made into a long drink with soda. The makers urge that it should always be served well chilled or with ice.

Vieille Cure. Made by the Company of Vieille Cure de Cenon, this is a liqueur based on herbs, the recipe purporting to contain at least forty different types of plant. These are macerated in both Armagnac and Cognac, and the result is a dark-coloured digestive.

Lillet. This is a pale, lightly aromatic wine-based apéritif, really a type of vermouth. It is made at Cenon, across the river from Bordeaux. Drunk straight, perhaps with a twist of lemon and well chilled, it is an extremely pleasant apéritif.

Cordial Médoc. A claret-based liqueur, this is dark red in colour, and on the sweet side, with some herb flavourings added to it. It is made by G. A. Jourde, Compagnie Fermière de Liqueurs, at Cenon.

Rhum. The enormous establishment of Bardinet has dominated the French *rhum* trade for well over a century, although in the near future, as it is now part of the gigantic Cointreau organisation, shipments are going to be made from Le Havre. Bardinet's best known product is Rhum Negrita, which is regarded as an almost essential bottle in the majority of French kitchens, where it is used not merely for flavouring, flaming and whipping into creamy puddings, but is much employed in pastry and sweet making. But the Bardinet establishment have a range of *rhums*, and anyone who has previously only sampled those popular in the U.K. will find the French *rhums* (the finer ones are produced in Martinique) very different in character, extremely fragrant and delicate, and the old liqueur *rhums* of remarkable elegance and finesse.

6

Gastronomy— the Food of the Region

Any meal of importance in the Gironde is wine-orientated: the bottles will be selected before the menu is decided. But the fare itself can be first-rate, usually rather simpler than the more obvious specialities of other regions, which may incorporate many sauces, much cream and a lot of general richness. Bordelais cooking is planned to set off the region's wines, never to draw attention from them or to conflict with them. This may be why I personally find it far less tiring and easier on the digestion, which may have been taxed after long sessions of tasting young wines. The quality of the ingredients can be superb. Of course, in the big hotels and luxury restaurants, which cater for tourists and all tastes, you will not always find the simpler and original versions of some dishes. But at smaller eating-places and in any private houses the local specialities bear only token resemblance to 'cuisine' and are usually what the British tourist happily recognises as 'good cooking'.

Wine in Restaurants

One thing that is worth bearing in mind: only in a very few restaurants nowadays will the wine list include clarets that the British customer will consider 'old'—that is, over ten years from their vintage date. In a good or great vintage, such wines may still be young, but the necessity for turning over stocks (which cost money to keep, even if only because they occupy space) and the general preference of many French customers for drinking such fine wines while they are, to a Briton, still far too young, has made this predominance of very young wines inevitable. The practice can be useful, for visitors can sample clarets that are still too young to be listed by U.K. merchants, and therefore be able to plan their prospective buying.

Fine old wines may be found—but they may, in a French restaurant, even in the Gironde, be more expensive than in a good or luxury eating place in the U.K. They will certainly tend to cost less at home if you buy your own wines and bring them to where you are dining, unless you are lucky enough to find some truly out-of-the-way cache in the Bordeaux region.

Nor should the traveller expect that wines will be handled as even the moderately informed wine waiter in the U.K. might produce them. It will usually be necessary in the Gironde to stipulate if you want a wine decanted and, if this is done, it may be a mere matter of just pouring an already disturbed wine into a decanter. Even in first-class hotels and restaurants, the careful and correct handling of wine tends to be as rare in the Gironde as it is in the U.K.

The traveller fortunate enough to be entertained by anyone in the wine trade will usually be favoured with at least one of the wines of either the estate belonging to or associated with the host, or else from the list of those that are the exclusivities or specialities of his firm. Naturally the guest will be appreciative and can, without offence, comment on these and other wines. But it should perhaps be borne in mind that a direct comparison of the host's wines with those of another estate or firm can be risky; there may be serious rivalry between the two estates, firms, or families involved, and even if the guest praises the host's wines above others, there may well be someone else present at a lunch party who may report elsewhere that So-and-So commented adversely on the wines of another establishment. Tongues wag around the decanters and the grapevine can spread gossip and criticism, both in Bordeaux and Britain, with satellite-like speed. So, when in doubt, praise, and don't compare, unless, of course, you are favourably comparing two wines both from the same house.

SEAFOOD

The Arcachon basin is the centre of an extensive amount of oyster cultivation, the oysters being attached to specially-shaped tiles in *parcs* or demarcated sections of this inland sea. There are two main kinds, the *gravette*, or local variety, which is a type of '*plate*' or flat oyster (*ostrea edulis*) such as the Briton will envisage and which has been cultivated in the Gironde since Roman times. The poet Ausonius commented that they were served at the beginning of banquets by Germanicus, nephew of Julius Caesar.

About 1920 the *gravettes* were seriously attacked by illness and from that time onwards Portuguese oysters, locally known as *noisettes*, augmented the supply. This *Portugaise* (*Crassostrea angulata*) is more oval than round, unlike the *plate* its shell is heavily ridged and deeper, and its flavour, although good, not as delicate. This type of oyster is supposed to have been brought back from India to Portugal by the explorer Vasco da Gama, because the oysters attached themselves to the hulls of his ships. In 1868 the sailing ship *Morlaisien*, en route to England with a cargo of Portuguese oysters, took shelter in a storm in the Gironde estuary near Pauillac; when the cargo became smelly, and the crew complained, the captain jettisoned it, thinking the oysters were dead. But some lived and began to thrive in the estuary, from which their cultivation spread.

Plates are sometimes referred to as *claires*, although strictly speaking a *claire* is an oyster park. Usually, the oysters are sold with the name of their place of origin attached: Marennes, or *verts* have a greenish colour, from certain seaweeds; '*belons*' are three-year-old *plates*, considered of the finest quality and with an *Appellation Contrôlée* to themselves. Oysters are sold according to size, usually from 4 down to o and oo—the lower the number, the larger the oyster.

On the shores near the oyster parks, oysters are always in season. It is only the hot weather and the difficulty of keeping them fresh that causes them to be reserved to months with an 'r' in them. The French way of serving them is usually by laying them, opened, on the flat part of their shell, whereas in Great Britain they usually rest on the hollowed part, so that the liquid can be drunk as well. In the Gironde they are often served accompanied by small, garlicky hot sausages, or slices of cold sausage or salami.

Other shellfish are freely available, and also snails, if they can be put into the category of crustacea, but possibly the most interesting local fishy speciality is the caviare of the Gironde. The long estuary of this river has made it fairly popular for sturgeon, and in 1918 Emile Prunier, founder of the famous Paris and London restaurants (of which the former still bears his name), was by then having difficulty in obtaining caviare from Russia because of the Revolution; so he thought that, in his native Gironde, the female sturgeon might provide an alternative supply. He brought a Russian from the Caspian Sea to teach the locals how to prepare the caviare: the result is a small-grained, finely-flavoured caviare, unfortunately expensive, but delicious.

The lamprey is another curious speciality and it too is only found in rivers with long estuaries, such as the Gironde. It is an invertebrate—that is, it has no backbone, only a long (and poisonous) vein down its back—and has a type of sucker at its head, with which it attaches itself to other fish to derive its nourishment. Lampreys were at one time strictly reserved for royal tables only, and they too are in shorter supply today. Henry I of England, the monarch unfortunately tagged with "died of a surfeit of lampreys", did succumb to an attack of indigestion and died in December 1135. But as this was in the Forest of Lyons, near Rouen, in Normandy, where the lamprey seems an unlikely local speciality, I wonder whether the King's food poisoning may not have resulted either from a lamprey 'gone off' even in the winter, or else one that had not had the poisonous back vein removed, by chance or design.

The flesh of the lamprey is a creamy colour and the flavour not very fishy—perhaps it might vaguely be described as being halfway between chicken and turbot. *Lamproie à la Bordelaise* is

Lampreys and wine

the lamprey, in pieces, cooked in an oil, butter and red wine sauce, with shallots, leeks, tomatoes, mushrooms, and seasonings; the eventual sauce looks very dark in colour and the dish is a rich one.

Petits Royans are sardines, which are sold either without salt, or salted. They are fished in many regions but at vintage time they are especially fat and succulent. There are also little river fish, *trogues*, rather like whitebait, which are sometimes found as *friture* in the country. But the great Gironde fish is certainly the *alose* or shad; this is a fish of a fairly large size, and it is also found in the Loire and also the Hudson River. Its flesh is of a very delicate flavour and the only disadvantage is that there are many fine bones. The *alose* may be served hot, grilled over vine prunings, or cold, with a sauce or vinaigrette dressing.

MEAT AND GAME

Pauillac lamb (*agneau de Pauillac*) is famous, though it should not be confused with *de près salés* (salty pastures) which is lamb-reared on the edge of the river (in the Gironde, it will usually come from the Charentes Maritimes). Remember that the French like their lamb undercooked so that it is pink, so ask for it *bien cuit* if you prefer it well done.

Beef in various forms is also often featured. Steaks are frequently cooked *aux sarments* (over the prunings of the vines) which gives a delicious flavour to the meat. An *entrecôte à la Bordelaise* is grilled in this way and served with beef marrow and shallots—the shallot (*echalote*) is to this corner of France what garlic is to the south-east and onions to the north. A *Sauce Bordelaise* is something quite different, sometimes—to the horror of purists—it is poured over an *entrecôte à la Bordelaise*. This sauce is of red wine, which, according to a large number of various recipes, may include red wine (or white for certain special variations), shallots, possibly beef marrow and various seasonings and different bases.

Game of the 'small feathered' type is abundent in the wine regions, and woodcock (*bécasse*), quails (*cailles*), larks (*alouettes*) and partridge (*perdreaux*) are all of excellent quality. Wild duck (*canard sauvage*) and wood pigeon (*palombe*) are other local game. Ortolans may be included here, although they are perhaps more a speciality of the Landes region, south of Bordeaux. Wheatears, tiny birds, used to be a great delicacy in England, and dishes for their service, with hollows rather like those on oyster plates, decorated with ears of wheat, are sometimes to be found in antique shops. Traditionally, the bones and head of the birds are eaten as well as the minute amount of flesh. One commentator says that the eater should cover his head with a napkin and simply gobble up the whole.

Two local dishes that I do not think are found elsewhere are the *gratons de Lormont*, a type of pounded pork and meat paste, somewhat similar to the rillettes of Touraine, but less fatty, and *foie de canard aux raisins*, a very rich recipe, involving the flambéeing of the duck livers and the mushrooms, grapes and seasonings with liqueurs.

There is also the local custom of *faire chabrot*. This means that, at the end of the service of a soup, such as any of the country recipes, the person eating may pour a little of the red wine in his glass into the remains of the soup and drink it up, as from a saucer or cup, without using a spoon.

At vintage time, those picking the grapes are carefully catered for—there is serious rivalry between the kitchens of the estates—and the *soupe des vendangeurs*, which contains generous quantities of meat and vegetables is excellent for assuageing hunger. Grills of meat *aux sarments* are also made, and, sometimes, in Bordeaux itself, the grills made for those working in the cellars (and their employers) may be cooked at the old fire-places in these establishments, where a fire may be made using the old cask staves, impregnated with wine. These, like the vine prunings, give a gorgeous flavour to the grills.

The outstanding vegetable of the region is the *cèpe*, of which one writer says "without *cèpes*, Bordeaux wouldn't be Bordeaux". The *cèpe* is a large mushroom, which may be cooked in various ways, but generally with oil, parsley, shallots (of course) and butter (only in Paris does garlic get involved with the recipe). *Cèpes*, however they are cooked, are rich and certainly one of the vegetables that should be eaten as a separate course, not with any meat or fish—and one portion of *cèpes* will usually suffice for two people. They have a particularly pungent aroma and great succulence.

There is a considerable amount of market gardening in the region, so that fresh vegetables are of excellent quality, but the artichokes of Macau are famous. The use of aubergines (and, for that matter, lamb *en brochette*) is considered by some to be an indication of the Moorish occupation of the area, but is more likely to be a recent importation from Algeria. The various culinary cultures that have affected the Gironde—Dutch, English, Spanish, Portuguese, German—have all left some traces in the dishes that remain. The regions adjoining Bordeaux, notably that of the Landes, the vast pine-forested area to the south, contribute also: the game, *foie gras*, (often served at the start of a meal with Sauternes, as our ancestors would have drunk it) and truffles of the Dordogne Valley, plus the hams of Bayonne, cured in a special way and matured by burying them in the ground. The liqueurs, as well as the wines of the region, notably the *rhums* of the French Antilles, and the *anisette* of Marie Brizard, are used in many dishes, especially for sweet recipes.

CHEESE

Curiously, there is no Bordeaux cheese. In the overall area, Queyrac makes a cow cheese, and Courpiac a goat cheese, but the Gironde is unusual in being a wine region without an accompanying cheese. Wine, especially red wine, tastes even better when it is served with a cheese, but although most good restaurants will be able to offer a selection of cheeses from other regions, the cheese that is eaten everywhere in Bordeaux is red-rinded Edam, known as *Holland*. The tradition for eating this with fine claret (with which it is admirable) seems to date from about the eighteenth century, when cargoes of Bordeaux wine were exchanged in Holland for consignments of the Dutch cheese. For visitors, the cheeses that seem to me to accompany fine claret will include the very creamy French cheeses, such as Brie (Camembert and Pont L'Evêque can be too strong), and anything that is 70–75 per cent *matière grasse* (stated on the label), also the goat cheeses, and the milder blue cheeses. Personally, I think that fine Roquefort is too strong for a delicate claret, but a Bleu de Bresse or really creamy Gorgonzola is possible or even a Danish Blue in prime condition. Those who love cheese and drink Bordeaux wines in the U.K. may also try the recommendation of the late Guy Prince, a great British shipper, who advocated the matured British hard cheeses, such as Cheddar or Lancashire, with the big sweet wines of Bordeaux—the combination is unusual, but not impossible; these cheeses are usually far too aggressive for the fine red wines, whereas the sweetness of the big Sauternes (such as one of the top classed growths) can partner them, oddly but effectively.

In a region where the wines dominate the table, the sweet course may be restricted to something simple, either a type of gâteau, or cake, or fruits. Fruits in wine, or in a syrup of wine or brandy are sometimes served. At St. Émilion, the macaroons are famous—smaller than in the U.K. but light and melting in the mouth—and there is also a recipe for *St. Émilion au Chocolat*, which is a type of chocolate mousse made with *rhum*.

Wine Tasting

There is nothing difficult about tasting wine, even if some people suppose it to be a mystery requiring a long initiation process! The aim of tasting is to discover an enjoyable wine, either enjoyable to drink immediately or likely to prove enjoyable after some period of maturation. When you visit a wine merchant's tasting or attend a tasting party, you are most likely to be offered samples of wines that are ready or very nearly ready to drink. When you visit a wine shipper, or anywhere in the region where wine is produced, you are more likely to get the chance of trying wines that are as yet not ready to drink. Indeed, some of the very finest wines do not make pleasant drinking at all while they are growing up and developing and there may be little temptation to swallow them. But although even a very little experience will acquaint you with different things to look out for in different wines at various stages in their development, the basic procedure of tasting is the same.

Wine is a beautiful and interesting commodity—and those who really know something about it and care for it are delighted to share their enjoyment and appreciation with even the humblest beginner as well as with the experienced. So do not be shy of trying to taste seriously. Ask questions and whenever possible try to note down your impressions of a wine *while* you are tasting it—even an hour later, your thoughts will lack precision. Also, if you remember in detail wines that you like or do not like your future shopping for wine is greatly helped. No-one wants to risk being a wine bore or wine snob, but the world of true lovers of wine is wide, hospitable and worthy of exploration.

Tasting Sense and Tasting Room Manners

The tasting room is the heart of the business of any wine establishment. Care is taken to ensure that the wines may be examined as critically as possible, and that nothing should interfere with this. It sometimes disappoints people to find that a tasting room is rather a clinical place, usually with a north light plus very strong artificial lighting, plenty of white on walls and benches against which the colours of wines may be examined, and with at least one sink and possibly several spittoons as well. But the 'picturesque' type of tasting is usually more in the nature of a party and not for the occasions when large sums of money are being allocated to the buying and selling of a firm's wines.

Visitors to the tasting room will naturally wish to conform to what may be described as 'tasting manners', by not making it difficult for anyone else to make serious use of the room either while they are there, or immediately after their visit. Scent and strongly smelling toiletries for men as well as for women should ideally be avoided or, if someone has just used scent or been on the receiving end of some pungent preparation at hairdresser or barber, it is worthy mentioning the fact by way of excuse, to show that you are aware this may be a distraction. Don't start to smoke, unless specifically invited to do so, as this may make the tasting room unusable for some while, though if the occasion is not too serious the host may well offer cigarettes in his office, if not actually in the tasting room. Beware of thinking that the shallow metal or enamel cups that often stand about in tasting rooms are ashtrays—they are tasting cups, and should not be casually used!

SHARING GLASSES

At professional tastings, unless someone has a cold, mouth infection or anything that obviously necessitates them keeping a single glass for their own use, it is usual for everyone tasting to do so from a single glass, which will be standing either in front of the bottle from which the tasting sample has been drawn or on a space marked in some way on the tasting bench. Some people are hesitant about sharing a glass, but may be reminded that wine is the second oldest disinfectant in the world. If you are really disinclined to taste from a glass used by anyone else, you should make no bones about asking for one for yourself.

Obviously, a woman does not want to leave lipstick on a wine glass at any time—it looks particularly revolting—and even a slight trace can affect the taste of the wine for anyone coming afterwards in a serious appraisal of wine. But it is a very simple matter to wipe the mouth before tasting, should anyone really be at the stage when they leave traces of lipstick on every eating utensil (quite unnecessary, if lipstick is correctly chosen and applied). Men should be reminded that, if they use strongly-smelling soap to wash their hands, or make use of pronouncedly fragrant aftershave lotion or any preparation for hair, they will make the glasses smell just as much as any woman's cosmetic.

A final piece of advice which may seem a little severe though is not so intended: anyone who is trying to form a precise opinion about a wine being tasted requires to be able to give that wine undivided attention. Anyone who, with a false idea of making themselves agreeable, insists on breaking in on the train of thought of the taster at such a moment, peering to see what notes have been written (the experienced taster usually evolves a shorthand which is quite indecipherable to anybody else) and generally making a noise of superficial or frivolous conversation, is likely to be more of a nuisance than a welcome guest in the tasting room. There are plenty of opportunities for asking questions and exchanging points of view without interrupting someone seriously at work, and—in case it should be thought that I am being unnecessarily stern—I must point out that some of the visitors to a tasting room may be those to whom the opportunity is both illuminating and of the greatest importance as regards their future approach to wine. To interfere with an opportunity that may come only rarely, or prevent someone from taking as much advantage as possible out of an experience of serious tasting is both selfish and boorish. The professional may be able to taste on another occasion: the visiting amateur may be deprived of a unique experience by the misplaced bonhomie of someone who really simply wants a drink and would therefore be better to cut short his visit to a tasting room and await the next stage of the proceedings outside.

SPITTING

In an age when virtually any subject can be discussed, it is astonishing that people still display hesitancy and even squeamishness about spitting out samples of wine that they are tasting. A moment's reflection will indicate that to spit out when tasting is the only sensible thing to do: not merely will the mixture of a number of different wines be confusing to the palate and probably upsetting to the stomach, but some samples may be out of condition, others, especially very young wines, undergoing some form of fermentation, and none of them may actually be enjoyable to drink. Spit them out. It is perfectly possible to eject wine from the mouth discreetly and without fuss. If you are tasting samples drawn direct from casks or vats in a cellar, it is usually acceptable to spit on the floor—remember that, if this is stone or cement, there will be some splashback, so try to avoid getting wine on your shoes or those of your companions. In the tasting room, the sink or spittoon will be sluiced down at intervals, even if there is not a tap running to keep everything fresh. Let me reiterate: spit out any samples offered for tasting, unless you are specifically given a portion of wine and advised to drink it. To swallow tasting samples risks giving yourself a stomach upset and will not improve your knowledge or experience of wine.

First Look at the Wine's Appearance

A tasting sample will only occupy a small space in the glass. Its appearance has much to reveal. Ideally, the glass should be perfectly clear and clean and on a stem, though in some regions you may have to make do with small tumblers or possibly a tasting cup of a special type.

The wine should be clear and bright, with something 'living' about it. Do not be concerned that there may be bits (known as 'flyers') in it, as these may be particles from a cask sample, which subsequent filtration may well remove. Their presence, very often, indicates a quality wine, and therefore they are not reasons for condemning the wine in any way.

Tilt the glass away from you at approximately an angle of 45°
and hold it against something white, so that you can examine the
colour. The living quality should be obvious, rather in the way
that the water of a spring is different from the flat dull water
drawn from a tap and left to stand for several days. Whether the
wine is red or white, it should be pleasant, ideally beautiful to
look at and give pleasure to the eye.

What the Wines Indicate by Colour

WHITE WINES

These tend to deepen in colour as they age, and, usually but by
no means invariably, the sweeter wines start their life by being
more golden than the pale light lemon gold of the drier wines. It
is also fairly safe to generalize to the extent of saying that white
wines from warm southern vineyards usually start by having a
more yellow-straw colour than those from very cold vineyards,
which will be pale lemon yellow, or almost very pale green. A
really old white wine (old in terms of its own maturity, not
specifically related to its age in terms of years) may assume
almost an orange tinge, reminiscent of some of the dry
Madeiras; this, and the sort of smell and taste that can come off
such wines result in the term 'maderised' often being applied to
them. It does not mean that they are undrinkable by any means,
but they will have changed their character.

Look, too, at the actual consistency of the wine in the glass.
The way in which it clings to the sides of the glass and trails
downwards with the pull of gravity can indicate a wine of great
quality if these trails (known as 'legs') are marked. This is also indicative of the glycerine content which will be marked in the
wines that naturally contain a certain sweetness.

RED WINES

Red wines tend to grow paler as they age, many of them being
purple-red at the outset. It is probably easier for most people to
see the different tones of colour in a red wine and it is helpful
sometimes to know that, with a very fine wine (whether you like it
or not) there tend to be far more distinct tones of colour visible
as you tilt the glass than in even a good cheap wine. Look at the
'eye' of the wine at the centre of the liquid, and then see the
gradations of colour out to the edge where the wine meets the
glass: a young red wine will be purplish down to black, with a
rim that may begin to lighten almost to a deep lilac tone. With a
little more maturity, it may become reddish and in the end a
beautiful crimson-orange with great age. Red Bordeaux
probably lightens more throughout its life than red Burgundy,
which tends to be very purple at the outset, except in certain
years when the colour can be on the light side.

Remember that, with all wines, age is relative. Some wines
show signs of great age when they are young in years, simply

because they are wines that should be at their peak while comparatively young and fresh; others, including the very greatest red wines and certain whites, remain apparently youthful for many years. Unfortunately, today's economic pressures make it necessary for many wine-makers to be able to mature their wines faster than in the past, so as not to tie up their capital; this means that a wine which you may have heard of as taking a long time to mature can be at its peak years before you expected this.'

Caution is advisable when appraising wines solely by colour, simply because the control of wine-making these days is a very skilled matter and has rightly been judged as important in the appeal a wine makes to its public. If you doubt this, get someone to prepare you two samples of the same red wine, one of them having some additional colouring in it, put there either with culinary colouring matter or by the addition of a few drops of a much darker wine. You will be surprised by the way in which you feel the darker wine to be more 'full-bodied' and possibly 'fruity'! Similarly, if you think that colour does not influence taste, try giving a critical appraisal of a wine out of a glass that is a dark definite colour, such as blue, green, or black: you will be astonished to find how, once one sense used in tasting is cut off, all the others are somehow distorted.

Smell the Wine

A wine should have a pleasant healthy smell, which, in certain wines, can be complex but which should always give enjoyment. You will release this and be able to sniff it more easily if you circulate the wine in the glass, holding the glass by the stem or, possibly, by the foot (not as difficult as it looks at the outset) and simply swinging the liquid round, putting your nose into the glass at intervals and sniffing. The aeration of the wine releases the fragrance.

Surprisingly, very few wines actually 'smell of the grape' although people often wish that they might! A few grapes, notably the Muscat, do possess a distinctive aroma, which is quite often easily identified as 'grapiness', but otherwise although certain grapes may result in wines smelling of those grapes, the associations with fruit are not always obvious. A wine should smell fresh and clean, but there are certain smells which, with young wines, may be present for a short time, indicating nothing more than that the wine is going through a phase of natural development.

These smells include the slightly beery smell which may mean the wine is still undergoing a stage of fermentation, a vaguely yeasty smell, which sometimes seems present when a wine has recently been bottled, a slightly sharp smell, often described as 'green', which may be present in even the best made wine in a year when the grapes have been unable to ripen perfectly. Or, in some instances, this green smell may mean that the vineyard contains a high proportion of young vines, the use of which is apparent in the early stages of the wine's development. Obviously woody smells can mean that the wine has been matured in new wood, this smell passing with time also, or, if the woodiness is of a soggy sort, it may mean that there is a faulty stave in the cask in which the wine has been matured.

You are unlikely to find 'corked' wine in a sample of a very young, bottled wine, but a complete absence of smell can be slightly sinister in this respect, indicating that something is preventing the wine from giving off its fragrance. It is the 'swimming bath' smell, reminiscent of chlorine, that is for me most definitely associated with corkiness—which, by the way, has nothing whatsoever to do with bits of cork being in the wine. Some people do find that corkiness reminds them of the smell of cork, but I have never been able to see this myself. A musty smell can be indicative of an ill-made wine, but it should not be confused with 'bottle stink'. This is the smell (that is often stale and flat) of the little quantity of air held in the bottle of wine under the cork, which may affect the taste of the first portion poured. A little aeration will cause this to pass very soon.

The good smells, interesting and pleasing to the nose, include a type of fruitiness, the different sorts of which will be associated with the various types of grape when the taster has gained a little experience. Young wines, especially those that are most enjoyable when drunk fairly young when they are at their peak of freshness, usually have an obvious fruity smell. Then there is a crisp almost sharp smell, like the freshness of a good apple, which can indicate the right kind of acidity balancing the fruit. This should be noticed in most young wines, especially those that are dry and light. Wines from cool vineyards tend to have more smell than wines from hot ones. The infinity of delicate, flowery, herby, and subtle depths of scent with which some of the great German and other northern vineyards are associated, and in the reds from vineyards where the vine has to struggle, such as Burgundy and Bordeaux, can be so beautiful, even while the wines are very young that, as is sometimes said, 'it is almost unnecessary to drink when the smell is so fascinating'.

With the finest wines, try to break up the general impression made on you by the smell into the first impact, anything that then reveals itself by further aeration, and finally see whether there appears to be some subtle, as yet unrevealed fragrance underneath the other smell. Wines are like people in this respect, the more obvious are not always the most rewarding. Sometimes, right at the end of a tasting, a smell can come out of a wine glass that may indicate something to look forward to in the future. Try to remain alert to register this if it is there.

Taste the Wine

Always adapt tasting techniques to what experience has taught you suits your own abilities best. But the most usual way to taste is to draw a very small quantity of wine—about a teaspoon-ful—into the mouth, accompanied by a small amount of air. There is no need to make a loud sucking noise while doing this, but the circumstance of pulling the wine into the mouth, plus some air, seems to sharpen up the impression it can make. Then circulate the wine in your mouth, pulling it over the tongue, letting it run along the sides of the mouth and getting a general 'feel' of what it is like: light/dry/sweetish/thick/thin/assertive/reticent/chewy/attaching itself to the sides of the mouth/attacking the gums (everyone's gums tend to ache after a lot of tasting!) Try to split up the numerous impressions which the wine may have to give you before you spit it out. Don't be hesitant about taking more than one sample in quick succession.

AFTER-TASTE AND FINISH

When you have tasted the wine and have spat out the sample, breathe out sharply—you will be aware of an extra smell, rather than a taste, that passes across the palate. This is the after-taste and it can reveal quite a lot about the wine: for example, it may be far more definitely fragrant than the original bouquet or smell, or it may have a lingering quality, known in wine terms as 'length', both of which can indicate that the wine has great promise and may develop considerably. Or there can be little or no after-taste, when a wine may be described as 'short'.

The way in which the wine leaves the palate is the 'finish'. Does it finish cleanly, or has it a trace of stickiness? Has it a final flourish of flavour, a definite extra touch of taste, or does it die away rapidly? The finish of any good wine, regardless of price, should be clean, and, with a fine wine, entice the drinker to take more. With a modest type of wine, the finish should at least refresh rather than cloy the palate.

THE WORK OF TASTING

Some people really do not like tasting young wines, and affirm that there is no point in doing so, as they are going to enjoy them when the wines are grown-up. This is quite true, but any musi-cian or artist is fascinated to see someone in the same line of business rehearsing or working. The way in which wines develop is equally fascinating; and, even though no-one would claim to know exactly what a wine was going to be like at its peak, any more than even the most experienced human being could judge of the detailed progress of another human's performance, the attempt to relate experience to what a wine is saying at one time or another and the backing of one's own judgment in hazarding a view as to the evolution of a particular wine is one of the most engrossing and challenging exercises. Make no mistake, tasting is hard work. It requires great concentration and results in real exhaustion if you have subjected yourself to a long session. The fact that it is, to a wine lover, perhaps the most exhilerating pursuit of all, is a compensation.

Remember what a particular wine has to give: a wine that should be dry ought not, in general, to lack acidity and be seemingly too sweet. A wine that is meant to develop over a period of years need not always be very amiable or even give very much impression of what it is going to be like, when it is in its early stages. A very fine wine usually makes some impression on the taster, though all wines can go through phases when they seem to smell and taste of very little. The medium priced and cheap wines are very difficult to taste: they can risk being very much alike, and experience is necessary to differentiate between their attributes and what may be their deficiencies.

Don't bother yourself with the game most wine lovers play of getting friends to 'taste blind' until you are a little experienced. It is perfectly true that this can be great fun and teach you an enormous amount, as the stark appraisal of a wine about which you know nothing at all can be a great test of your own honesty, courage and relation of the power of your taste memory. The fact that some people, on some occasions, can identify a wide range of wines with complete accuracy, is not, by itself, a tribute to more than the luck of the day and their considerable experience; they can be equally mistaken, with reasons for being so, on other occasions. The beginner can easily be discouraged by making apparently pointless mistakes, so that it is wise not to indulge in this until you have a little general knowledge of wines.

Meanwhile, it is only sense to bear in mind that you are unlikely, for example, to be offered a range of red Bordeaux in the tasting room of a Burgundy shipper or vice versa! Nor, in one wine region, are you likely to be offered a wide range of wines from several other districts. The visitor to Bordeaux who was disappointed in not seeing where 'the sherry wines were made' is not unique! Although a firm may handle a vast range of wines, it is unlikely that the visitor will ever be asked to taste more than one type at a time. What they are offered over a hospitable table, of course, may be very much wider in scope.

Taking Notes

Notes made on the spot are far more valuable than any general impressions recorded even a short time afterwards, but it is extremely difficult to translate taste impressions into words. To put 'good' or 'bad' is really equally useless—how do you know? It may simply be that the wine in question does or does not appeal to you at that stage of your experience. Try, whenever possible, to differentiate between wines that you truly like and wines that you may admire as good but which do not particularly appeal to you. I would recommend any taster to make up his or her own set of tasting terms as far as possible. It is useless making play with technicalities only half understood from books or to use terms which may mean something to one taster but very little to another. With even slight experience, it is possible to translate your own tasting impressions into language that may be generally understood, but if it helps you, for example, to write 'carnations' or 'violets' against a particular type of wine, then do so. You associate this wine with those particular flowers and no-one else is obliged to do so. But, if, merely because someone who seems to be authoritative, insists that 'wild thyme' or 'scrubbed oak table' is inevitably associated with a particular wine, do not attempt to agree with them unless you can wholly associate yourself with the experience—it is worthless if you cannot share it, and your own impressions will be more valuable to you if you can make the effort to formulate them in terms that enable you to remember what you taste.

Always date your tasting notes and be precise about where the tasting was done, if you are not using a tasting sheet provided by the establishment. It is surprisingly easy, especially if the wines are good and seem to become better and better, for the impression at the end of any tasting to be wonderful but confused!

Deterrents to Tasting

There are a few things that make it difficult to taste. Some— smoking, scent, etc.—have been mentioned earlier. Obviously, a cold prevents you from doing so easily, and very few people find it easy to taste after they have had a large mid-day meal. The morning, when the stomach is fairly empty and both the mind and body are fresh, is probably the ideal time. Otherwise, if you wish to prepare your palate for serious tasting, remember that violently flavoured or piquant foods can make it difficult for you, and this should also be remembered when you are choosing wines to go with a meal. Of course, few people would be silly enough to eat curry, large amounts of pickles, or anything containing a high proportion of vinegar while trying to drink a fine wine, but other things can impair the receptivity of the palate, notably eggs and chocolate. Indeed, a single chocolate makes it almost impossible for me to taste for several hours afterwards! Anything very sweet, or a piece of confectionery, will also make it quite impossible to taste for some time—even a medium dry wine will taste incredibly acid after such a thing.

People are sometimes offered crusts of dry bread or biscuits to refresh the palate at a tasting, but there is one thing that you will never accept if you are being serious about the procedure—cheese. Not for nothing do the wine trade say 'we buy on apples, sell on cheese', because the alkalinity of cheese has the effect of making almost any wine taste better than it may perhaps be, whereas the acidity of an apple, or a crisp young carrot, will show up a wine quite brutally for good or bad.

Glossary
of Wine Terms

The following vocabularies gives certain terms that may be either difficult to find in a dictionary or, if they are given, will there bear a different significance from that which they carry in the world of wine. It is pertinent to remark that, from region to region, the terms will vary and that, say, a visitor from another French wine region may find the specialised use of certain expressions and words peculiar to the Bordelais. (Words and phrases used in relation to travel, especially driving, can be found in any of the motoring guides issued by the various associations such as the AA and RAC, and there are numerous publications that give detailed menu and restaurant terms and names). I have divided the vocabulary into the sections in which the particular words and phrases may be heard—obviously, someone whose French is good will assimilate them and use them in French conversation. But somebody being shown a vineyard will probably find even the experienced English-speaking guide may use local terms, which may be difficult to translate; likewise, in the *chai* or tasting room, if a conversation includes such an unfamiliar term, then the visitor may fail to understand the rest of what is being said. So, for quick reference, the aspects of the subject are divided up.

It is quite easy, with those who are in sympathy about a subject, for somebody to understand what is being said in a language that the hearer cannot actually speak—therefore the importance of knowing some of the trade or local terms is obvious; one can ask a question in English and receive the answer in French—if the key words and phrases are able to be explained.

There is also the matter of certain expressions being understandable but not translatable! '*Un vin fin*' is not, at all, the same thing as 'a fine wine', any more than '*un grand vin*' is really 'a great wine'. This is where the 'understanding of the heart' must come in, for the shades of meaning and the associations of certain phrases in any language cannot be submitted to any exact translation in words. But it should be borne in mind that here the terms are used as they would be in the Gironde—as I would use them talking to friends. In other parts of France slightly different meanings may be attached to them.

People

Un propriétaire An owner of a vineyard.

Un fermier A peasant farmer—not to be confused with *un propriétaire*, who is the overall proprietor.

Un régisseur A manager (of an estate); a bailiff.

Un maître de chai A cellarmaster, who directs the vineyard routine in detail and makes the wine.

Un vigneron A vineyard worker.

Un courtier A (wine) broker.

Un négociant eleveur A shipper. Often shortened to the first word only.

Un marchand de vin A wine merchant. In France this usually means a small-scale distributor. Elsewhere, of course, it may refer to a merchant or merchant-cum-shipper as the term is understood in the U.K.

Vineyard terms

Une propriété A property (an estate).

Un vignoble A vineyard.

Le terrior Type of soil—i.e. terrain.

Soils

Aliotique Alios, a type of sandstone peculiar to the south-west of France.

Argile Clay.

Calcaire Limestone.

Craie Chalk.

Croupe A ridge or slight elevation in the ground.

Gravelleux Gravelly.

Palus The riverbank vineyards of the Gironde estuary, not nowadays producing fine wines.

Sable Sand

Sous-sol Subsoil—very important, as it affects both the drainage of the vineyard and the source from which the long taproots of each vinestock obtain their nourishment.

Vines

Le cépage Vine variety, species, as when used to determine the type of grape. *Quel cépage?*—What kind of grape variety?

Coulure A type of vine disease that makes the grapes drop off their stalks.

La fleuraison The flowering of the vine (in the spring).

La grappe The cluster of grapes in a whole bunch.

Greffer To graft; the *porte greffe* is the stock of disease-resistant type of vine onto which the specific type of wine vine required is grafted

La grêle Hail, which can destroy an entire crop in minutes, and scar the vineshoots. Not to be confused with *le gel*, which is frost (*geler*—to freeze).

Pourriture Rot. *Pourriture grise* is ordinary grey rot, but *Pourriture noble* is noble rot—by the action of which the great sweet wines are made.

La souche The vinestock. To buy *sur souche* is the colloquial expression for buying before the vintage, on the expectation of the probable harvest and the past reputation of the estate—i.e. to buy 'on spec'.

Tailler To prune (most Bordeaux vines are pruned according to *la taille Guyot*).

La tige The stalk.

Les vendanges The vintage (in the autumn).

Wine making

La bonde The bung. *Bonde dessus*—Bung upwards (i.e. on the upper side of the cask, so that gas from the wine that is still fermenting can escape). *Bonde de côté*—bung on the side (i.e. when the bung has been driven home and the cask is turned so that the wine continues its fermentation in wood sealed from contact with the air).

Une barrique A cask—possibly best translated in the Bordeaux region by the word 'hogshead' (see page 32).

Une cave A cellar. The implication is that this is underground, either in the home of somebody, or else that the term relates to the stocks held by a shipper. The word can also be used to refer to the actual contents of the cellar—for which the English word 'stock' is also often used: e.g. *Il a des stocks formidables dans ses caves*—He's got impressive reserves in his cellars.

Un chai A storage place for wine at ground level. The term is used elsewhere, but is particularly associated with Bordeaux, as the nature of the terrain means that below-ground cellars can seldom be excavated, the water-table in the Médoc in particular being too high, and even the actual cellars in Bordeaux itself seldom being more than just below ground level. At an estate, there will usually be the *chai* for the new wines and a *chai* for those maturing in their second year, the two being collectively known as *Les chais*.

Coller To fine. The process whereby particles in suspension in wine are removed and the wine is clarified. The process of fining should not be confused with that of filtration, or racking.

Couper To blend (the verb actually means 'to cut'). *Faire le coupage*—to do the blending. The term was translated literally in English right up to the present century, when British customers would ask for their clarets 'cut' with other wines to up the strength and increase colour and toughness.

Une cuve A vat. *Une cuvée* is the contents of the vat—a vatting. *La cuverie* or *Le cuvier* is the building that houses the vats—i.e. a vathouse, where the wine is made. The dictionary gives *Cuver*—'to ferment', but I have never known the verb used in this way; one would say *fermenter*, or, if tasting a wine that is still fermenting, *Il travaille*—It's (still) working.

Débourbage Process of handling white wines in use on many estates today (see page 35).

Egrapper To de-stalk. *Un égrappoir* or, more fully, *Un égrappoir fouloir* is a de-stalking appliance. *Egrappage à main* is the process whereby the grapes are rubbed off the stalks by hand (see page 29).

Chaptaliser To add sugar to the must, so as to assist the process of fermentation in a poor year (see page 30).

Le chapeau The 'hat' or mass of grapeskins, pips and general debris that rests on the top of the must in the vat during fermentation.

Égalisage The process whereby the different vattings of wine, which are usually run off into cask as the process of fermentation in the vat finishes, are then blended to achieve the *grand vin* (see pages 32–3).

Fermenter To ferment.

Filtrer To filter.

La mise en bouteilles The bottling process. Often shortened to *La mise*, e.g. *Quand allez-vous faire la mise?*—When are you going to do the bottling?

Le moût The must—the grapejuice before it has become wine through the process of fermentation.

Le pressoir The press—in this context, used generally of the type of press that actually squeezes any remaining juice out of the debris finally left in the vat (see page 31). If a specific type of press (*Une presse*) such as that operated with chains inside (page 35) or by an inflated bag (page 35), then this will be referred to by the name, either of its type, or that of the manufacturer (*Une presse Seitz*, for example). A *pressoir* is essentially an old type of press, operated by the turn of a screw. *Vin de presse* is the result of this kind of pressing and, although in some years the first liquid resulting from the pressing may be added to the main wine being produced, to assist with its constitution by means of the extra tannin or other elements, this is not always so, and the *vin de presse* may be reserved for domestic use and not sold (see page 31). The term *vin de presse* used in a general way would be rather pejorative—implying that the dregs of the vintage had been used to make the wine

La récolte The crop—i.e. the yield (of grapes). Term often used to signify the vintage, e.g. *Une bonne récolte*—a good harvest.

Soutirer To rack—i.e. draw wine off from its lees, usually done by pumping it from one cask to another (see page 32).

Velenche This word does not feature in any dictionary and therefore, although I assume it is feminine, I do not know. It is the syringe-like instrument with which wine is drawn from the cask, the *velenche* being inserted through the bunghole and then, when the whole of the *velenche* is filled by the wine coming in through its nozzle, the thumb stops the hole at the other end so that the filled cylinder (either glass or metal) can be lifted free of the cask. Slight relaxation of the pressure by the thumb can then direct a stream of wine into a glass for tasting. Also sometimes referred to as *La pipette*.

Vinifier The process whereby grape juice is turned into wine—to vinify. Not to be confused with *Viner*—To add alcohol to wine. *Un vin viné* is what English-speaking people would term a fortified wine, whereas a *vin bien vinifié* is 'a well-made wine.'

Casks and bottles

Une barrique A cask, but, in Bordeaux, one of specific size (47–49 gallons, 221 litres), possibly best translated as 'hogshead'.

Un fût A cask, of any kind, sometimes used of one that is empty.

Un tonneau A cask holding about 4 hogsheads, but, nowadays, the term is generally used as a measure, and the word is used to indicate the production of an estate in reference works.

Un bouchon A cork. *Un tire-bouchon* is a corkscrew.

Une étiquette A label.

Une bouteille fantaisie An unusual bottle, such as may be specially put out for a special presentation or tourist souvenir.

Tasting

Un crachoir A spittoon (*Cracher* is 'To spit').

Déguster To taste.

Le millésime The vintage date. *Un vin millésimé* is a vintage wine'. *Un grand millésime* is 'a great vintage'.

Un vin fin Signifies something more than 'a fine wine'—perhaps 'a wine of marked quality'.

Bien equilibré Well balanced—signifying that the components of the wine unite harmoniously.

Corsé Full-bodied.

Un vin de garde A wine worth keeping.

Avaler To swallow or gulp down, differing from *Boire*—'To drink'.

Jolie robe Comment when a wine has a beautiful colour.

Bouqueté Fragrant.

Net, nette Clean, sound, flawless.

Further Reading

The problem about recommending books on such a constantly changing commodity as wine is that, within a short time of publication, the rules controlling its production may have altered, the information about certain aspects of the wine may be out of date, new discoveries may have been made and wines previously unfamiliar or only known to a few may be making history. Nor is it generally helpful to recommend books that have been out of print so long that they may be difficult for the ordinary reader to consult.

As regards Bordeaux, a great deal has been and is being written. Some authors, interesting for their place in wine writing history, are not cited here, either because what they wrote has now little relevance to the public's approach to the wines of Bordeaux, or because their books contain statements that might be misleading, and even inaccuracies that ought to have been checked at the time of writing or publication.

If you have a favourite general wine book, it is worth bearing in mind that no one writer can know everything about even one wine—so, however helpful and reliable you find a particular author, you should also see what others have to say. Some people prefer a strictly factual book, others opt for anecdotal and personal styles of writing. If you read French, there are many more books available. This list is limited to those that may usually be bought in the U.K. without difficulty and consulted even by those who might not otherwise think of making use of a book in French.

Bordeaux et ses Vins, Ch. Cocks & Ed. Feret (Feret et Fils, Bordeaux) is a compilation of all the Bordeaux wine estates, with relevant data as to production, plus information about the various regions and particulars as to the nomenclature of the wines of each. The last edition is that of 1969, so inevitably it is somewhat dated, but Cocks & Feret is the indispensable reference work for the serious student of Bordeaux. The French is not very difficult.

Côte de l'Atlantique, in the Michelin series of Green Guides is possibly the best overall regional general guide and brief sections on wine and gastronomy are included. Much of the information is given in table or statistical form, and the French text should be acceptable to anyone who has slightly more than an elementary knowledge of the language.

The Wines of Bordeaux, by Edmund Penning-Rowsell (Penguin) is certainly the most important contemporary work on the subject, dealing with history, details of production of the main estates of all the Bordeaux regions and the author's personal impressions of the wines. It is invaluable for reference.

The Great Wine Châteaux of Bordeaux (Times Books) is a finely produced pictorial record of the best-known properties, with background history and contemporary comments by a young Dutch journalist.

For general reference *The Wine Companion* (Collins) by David Burroughs and Norman Bezzant is extremely useful, Alexis Lichine's *Encyclopaedia of Wines & Spirits* (Cassell) is larger and more detailed, *The Penguin Book of Wines* (Penguin) by Allen Sichel, revised by Peter Sichel, is a classic approach to wine by a particular authority on Bordeaux, and Hugh Johnson's *World Atlas of Wine* (Mitchell Beazley) contains superb detailed maps of the region, with the author's comments on the wines and a very useful section on Bordeaux in general. My own *The Taste of Wine* (Macdonald & Jane's) is concerned throughout with many Bordeaux wines, of which there is a detailed personal comment in the section on tasting.

The Wonder of Wine by Edouard Kressmann (Hastings House, New York) is a charming and wise approach to the wines of Bordeaux, by one of the most respected members of a great wine dynasty. The personal reminiscences added to the practical advice makes this the nearest thing in print to enjoying the hospitality of a Bordeaux shipper. *Bordeaux and Aquitaine* by Lyn Macdonald (B. T. Batsford) is generally about the region, with advice on tours throughout, plus suggestions as to what to eat where, and general comments on wines and how they are made. *Lafite* by Cyril Ray (Peter Davies) is an account of this great estate by a most elegant and erudite author. *His Mouton-Rothschild* (Christie's Wine Publications) deals with this other famous first growth.

Appellation Contrôlée

This term, which is abbreviated to either A.C. or A.O.C., is in full *Appellation d'Origine Contrôlée*. It is a system of controls as to where and how certain wines are made. In 1935 a decree law, referred to as the Capus Law after the senator who drew it up, eventually led to the establishment of the *Institut National des Appellations d'Origine des Vins et Eaux-de-Vie*. This is generally referred to by its initials—I.N.A.O. This government-appointed body is supported by a small levy on each hectolitre of wine vintaged in France, and it exerts a strict control on all wines and spirits to which the A.C. is or may be granted. As no Bordeaux wines are of lesser standing than A.C., it is important to know the meaning of the term.

An A.C. is granted by I.N.A.O. subject to application, and each A.C. is an individual award to the area which it concerns; the local wine syndicates work out the conditions as to what the wines should be like, how cultivated and from which area. In addition, the A.C. is subject to the granting of the *label*, a word which, in French, signifies rather more than the English word 'label', and which is awarded annually as the result of the actual tastings held by the local syndicates.

The A.C. regulations define:

The exact area in which the vineyard is.

The variety or varieties of vines that are planted.

The method whereby the vines are trained and pruned.

How many vines planted per hectare (a hectare, often abbreviated to 'ha.', is 2.471 acres).

The minimum amount of sugar that is in the 'must', or unfermented grape juice.

The minimum degree of alcohol that is in the finished wine.

The maximum production of wine permitted, expressed in hectolitres (1 hectolitre is often abbreviated to the word 'hecto.' and is about 22.4 gallons) per hectare.

How the A.C. works

Many people believe that the possession of the right to put

'A.C.' on the label of a wine guarantees its quality. This is not and cannot be so, even although all the fine wines of France are now A.C. wines. But, on reflection, you will appreciate that it would be possible for a wine to be 100 per cent exactly what it should be according to the A.C. requirements, and still not necessarily be a good or fine wine. The quality of a wine can be only implicitly associated with the A.C. The only factors that can establish and maintain a wine's quality are the conscientiousness of the man who grows the vines and makes the wine, and, as far as the customer is concerned, the scrupulousness of the man or men who care for the wine after it is made, bottle it and transport it to wherever it is going to be drunk.

The other thing that people do not always understand is that A.C.s fit inside each other, and that any old A.C. shouldn't suffice if you really want to know what a wine is—and, by implication, what it may be like. For example, a wine that is merely A.C. *Bordeaux Rouge* is only required to attain a minimum degree of 10° of alcohol, whereas a *Bordeaux Rosé* or *Bordeaux Clairet*, both of them pink wines, must be 11° and a red *Bordeaux Supérieur* must be 11.5°. Yet, at the top of the aristocracy of the Médoc, the minimum degree of alcohol required for all the parishes (communes) is 10.5°, and, for the A.C.s *Haut-Médoc* and *Médoc*, 10°. The A.C.s are equally strict as regards the white wines. In certain regions, the use of certain vine varieties is restricted to a percentage for the area.

There are also some alternative permitted A.C.s, which may be put on the labels when the wines are sold. This relates particularly to those that may, because of perfectly straightforward but unforseen circumstances, have exceeded the permitted quantity of wine per hectare. The other form in which wines are 'declassified' (nothing to do with the system of classification of different areas), occurs when, maybe only in one small area, even at a single estate, a wine is made that the authorities do not consider deserving of the higher-ranking A.C. and they declassify to an A.C. of a more general type—*Médoc*, *Bordeaux Supérieur*, or even just *Bordeaux*.

It is also essential to remember that some of the finest wines of the Médoc are outside the specified (delimited) regions entitled to an A.C.: Macau, for example, has no A.C. to itself, and therefore the invariably fine wines of Château Cantemerle, a classed growth, and also the various bourgeois growths of this parish, bear only the A.C. '*Haut-Médoc*'. The same applies to Château La Lagune in Ludon, as Ludon has no A.C.

But, to simplify the system for the benefit of the visitor to the Bordeaux region, or for anyone drinking its wines, the label of the wine should bear the A.C. of its particular area. For example, there are a number of estates that are entitled to bear the name of Latour: seven, with the word as given, seventy-nine as 'La Tour'; true, the 'Latours' have some form of suffix in the words that come after the first word, and the 'La Tours' likewise, but there is only one Château Latour that is A.C. Pauillac—and that is the great first growth. Wine lovers who think they are getting this first growth when what they have may be a good but not comparable wine, merely called 'Latour something-or-other', should look at the A.C., and then they won't write cross letters to people like me saying that the wine was less expensive than what they would have been charged for "the" Latour and why don't I "expose" exorbitant pricing?

It will, clearly, be understood that wines such as Château Latour or Château Margaux bear A.C.s that clearly indicate exactly what they are: the A.C. *Pauillac* for Château Latour, and that of *Margaux* for Château Margaux make it impossible to confuse them with any wine from another estate in another area.

If someone uses the name of the château without the prefix 'château' there can be some confusion—I have known people tell me that they were drinking "Margaux" when in fact they were drinking the generic wine of the region, not, certainly, that of the great first growth estate. But it is not really difficult to sort out A.C.s if you think of them as versions of pedigrees, establishing where a wine comes from and what, essentially, it is—not necessarily, however, how good it is, any more than an animal or human pedigree can do so. Thus, a label telling you that a wine is from Château Lafite will be A.C. Pauillac—the Lafite estate is within the parish (*commune*) of Pauillac, which has its own A.C. Pauillac, however, is within the region of the Haut-Médoc, which is within the overall area of the Médoc, and this inside the category of Bordeaux Supérieur—and, of course, Bordeaux. But the more defined the region, the more superior the A.C. Incidentally, the term *supérieur* does not, in this context, imply superiority of quality, but a stricter sort of A.C.

Here are the A.C.s of the areas of the Bordeaux region: St. Estèphe, Pauillac, Saint-Julien, Moulis, Moulis-en-Medoc, Listrac, Margaux, Haut-Médoc, Médoc. These are all red wines and the A.C.s can also be Bordeaux Supérieur and Bordeaux.

The white wines are: Cérons, Barsac, Sauternes, Graves, Graves Supérieures; the other A.C.s that may be used are Graves Supérieures (for Cérons), Sauternes (for Barsac), Bordeaux Supérieur for Cérons, Barsac and Sauternes, and Bordeaux for all of them. Of course, red Graves are made and bear the A.C. Graves. But it is interesting that the dryish white Sauternes and Barsacs produced at many estates are, by the A.C. regulations, only allowed to bear the A.C. Bordeaux Supérieur, because the regulations established that, for the A.C.s Sauternes or Barsac, the wines have to be sweet.

Sainte-Croix-du-Mont, Loupiac, Côtes de Bordeaux Saint-

Macaire, and Premières Côtes de Bordeaux, followed by the names either Cadillac or Gabernac, or Premiéres Côtes de Bordeaux followed by the name of a parish (*commune*) not that of either of the previous two; then the red Premières Côtes de Bordeaux plus a specific parish name, Premières Côtes de Bordeaux red, and Premières Côtes de Bordeaux white. And there are the other A.C.s that may be used—Bordeaux Supérieur and Bordeaux.

Sainte-Foy-Bordeaux, Graves de Vayres, both making red and white wines, with the other A.C. Bordeaux.

Entre-Deux-Mers, Entre-Deux-Mers-Haut Benauge, Bordeaux Haut-Benauge, with another A.C. Bordeaux.

Bordeaux-Côtes-de-Castillon, Bordeaux Côtes de Francs, and Saint-Émilion (1er grand cru classé, grand cru classé and grand cru); the Saint-Émilions may simply have the A.C. Saint-Émilion if not the higher one, and all, including the following, may also have the A.C. Bordeaux Supérieur and Bordeaux: Saint-Émilion, Sables-Saint-Émilion, Montagne-Saint-Émilion, Lussac-Saint-Émilion, Parsac-Saint-Émilion, Saint-Georges-Saint-Émilion, Puisseguin-Saint-Émilion, Pomerol, Néac, Lalande de Pomerol, Côtes de Canon-Fronsac, Côtes de Fronsac.

Bourg, Côtes de Bourg, Bourgeais make red and white wines, the reds may have the lower A.C. Bordeaux.

Premières Côtes de Blaye making red and white wines may also have an A.C. Bordeaux or Blayais.

Côtes de Blaye making white wines may also have the A.C. Blayais.

Blaye or Blayais, making red and white; no other A.C.

The other A.C.s are: Bordeaux Supérieur, both red and white, Bordeaux Rosé or Clairet, and Bordeaux, both red and white.

Does all this seem to complicate the enjoyment of the wines? In fact it shouldn't—the A.C. pinpoints the exact area, which, if a parish (*commune*), makes it simple to find the whereabouts of the property. If the A.C. is of a larger area than just a parish, then the characteristics of this area will be noted in the wines anyway. If some of them are in fact the declassified wines of an estate, which for technical reasons (such as excess of production, for which the French word is *rendement*) or something similar that makes it impossible for the wine to bear the label of the higher A.C. then the wine may still be excellent value and of interest.

Keep in mind that any A.C. is an indication of what its name implies—where the wine comes from and how it was made. The name of the grower, the shipper and the merchant are the possible clues to how good it may be or, indeed, how much to your personal liking, for it is possible for a wine to be admittedly excellent—and you still don't care for it. I myself do not like the most famous 'great' years of one of the first growths. You can hardly be criticised for expressing a personal preference, even while owning that the wine concerned is extremely fine. This particular wine just isn't my idea of what I want from fine claret.

Index